I0409402

A true artist is not one who is inspired, but one who inspires others.

SALVADOR DALI

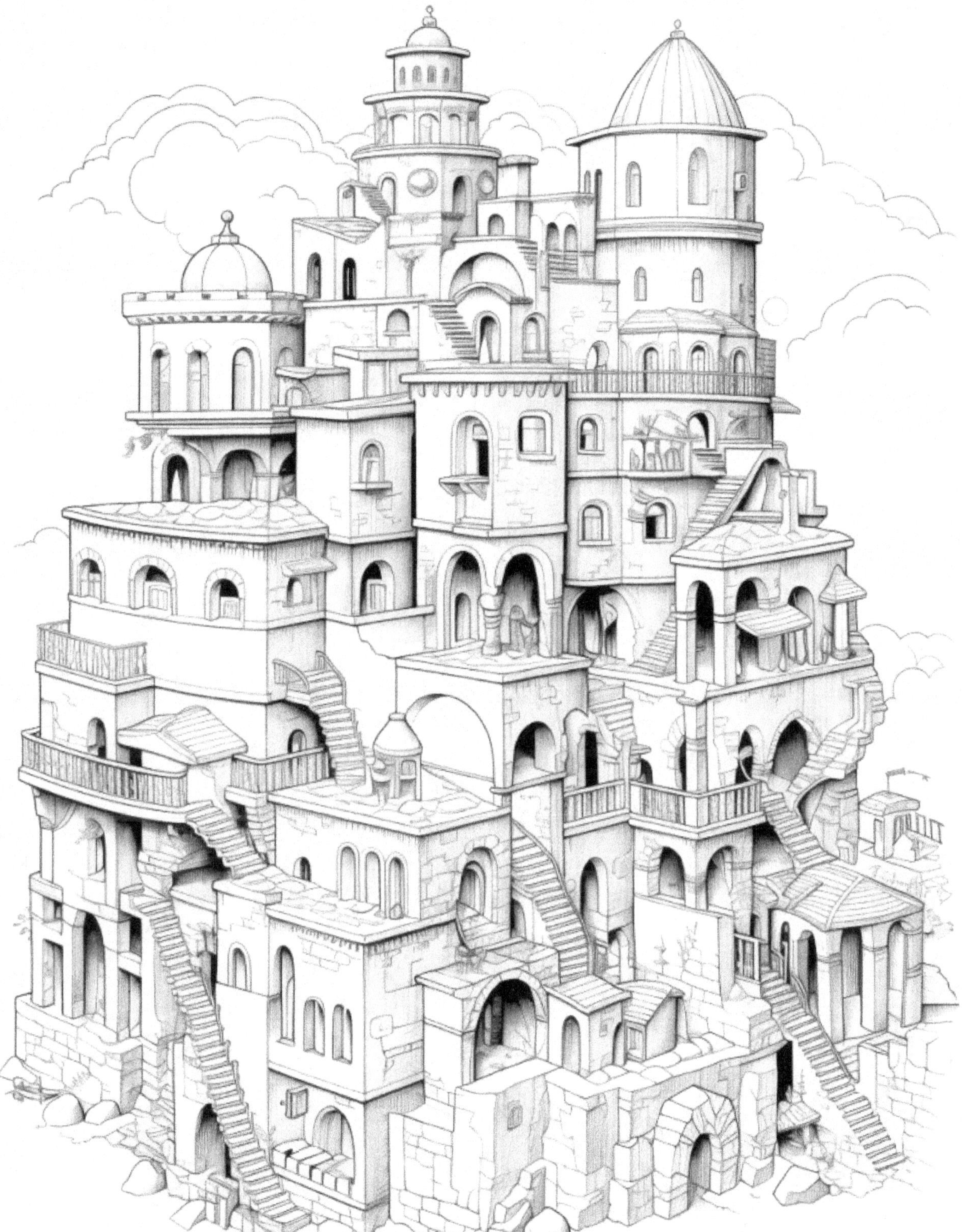

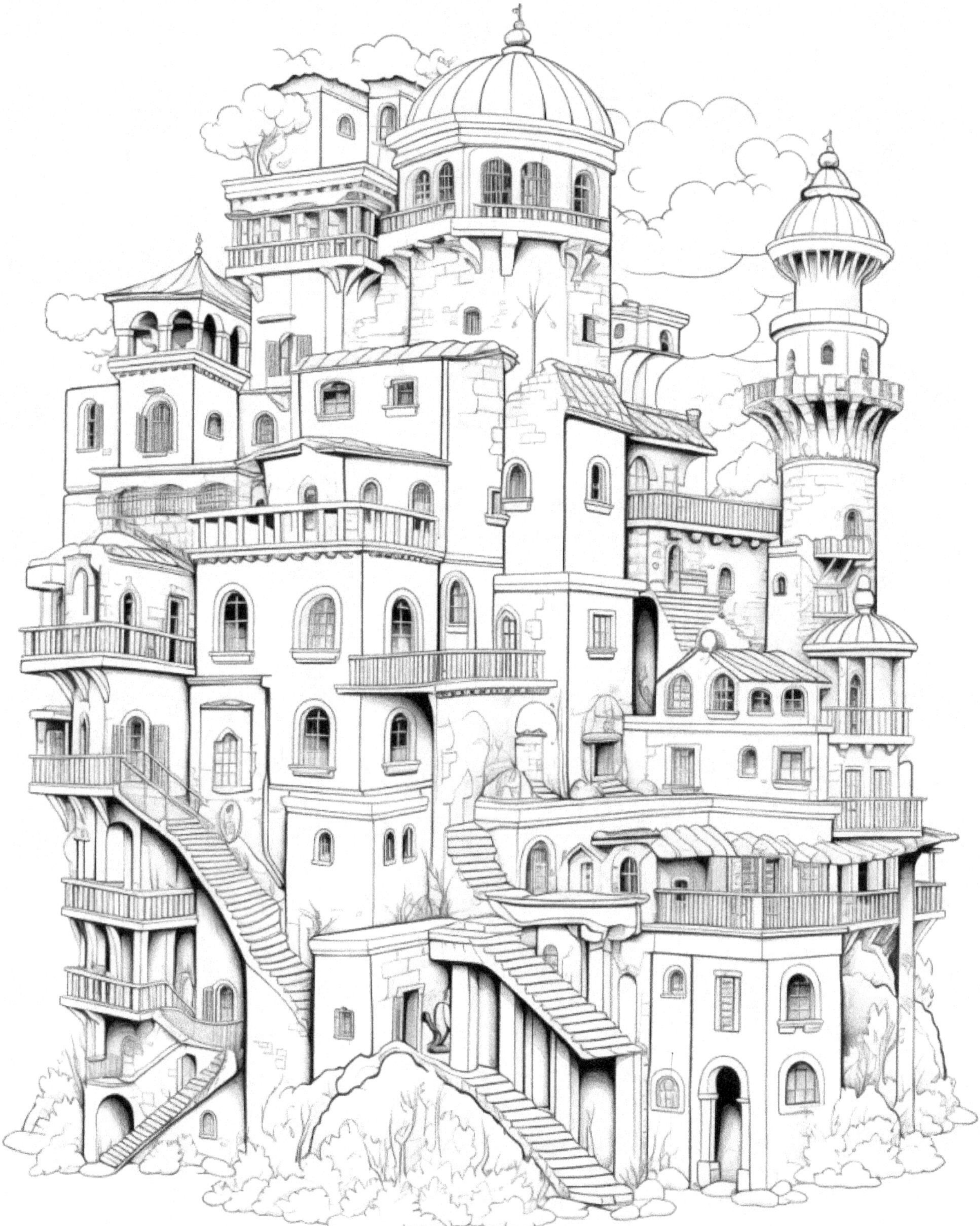

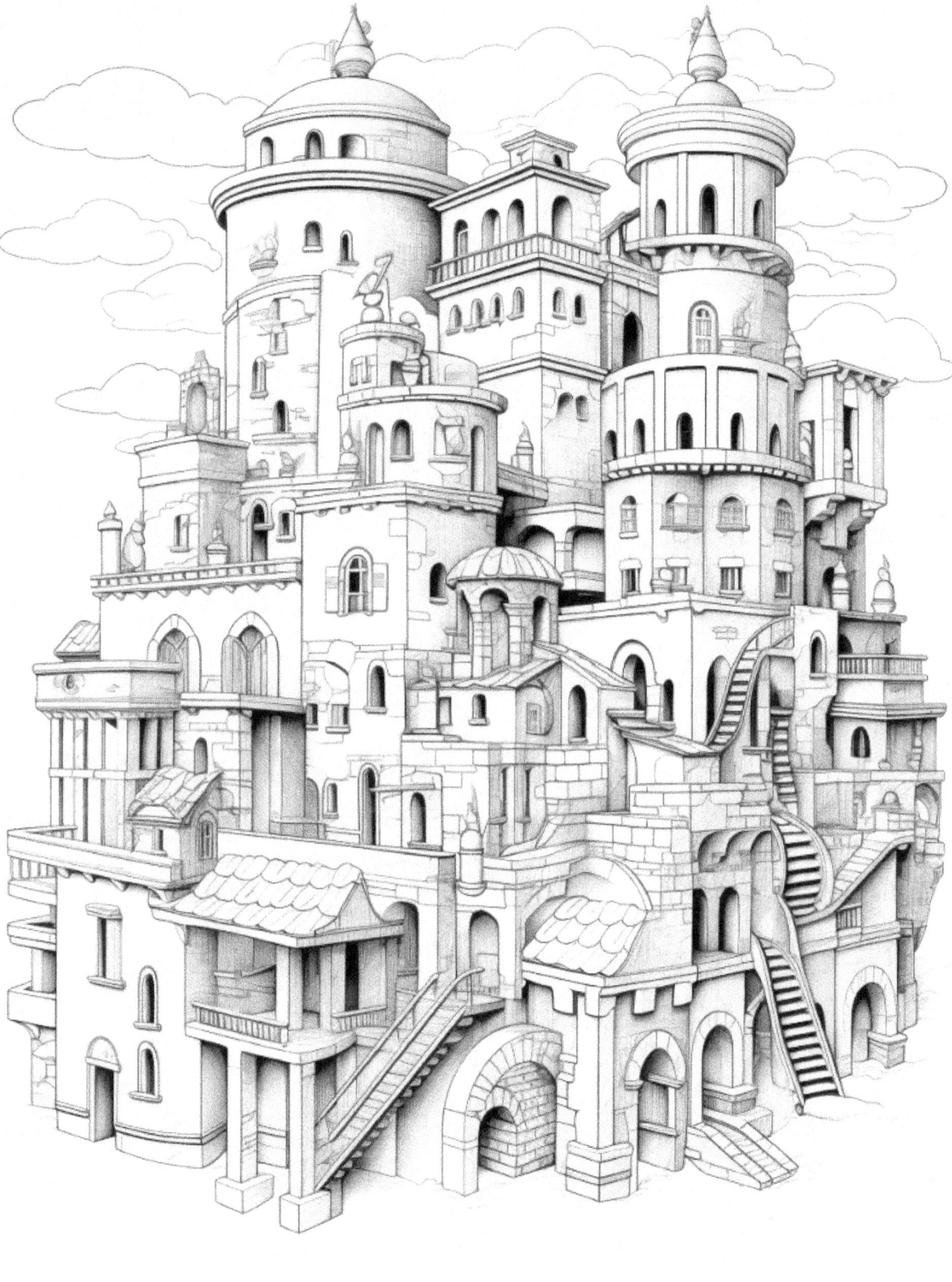

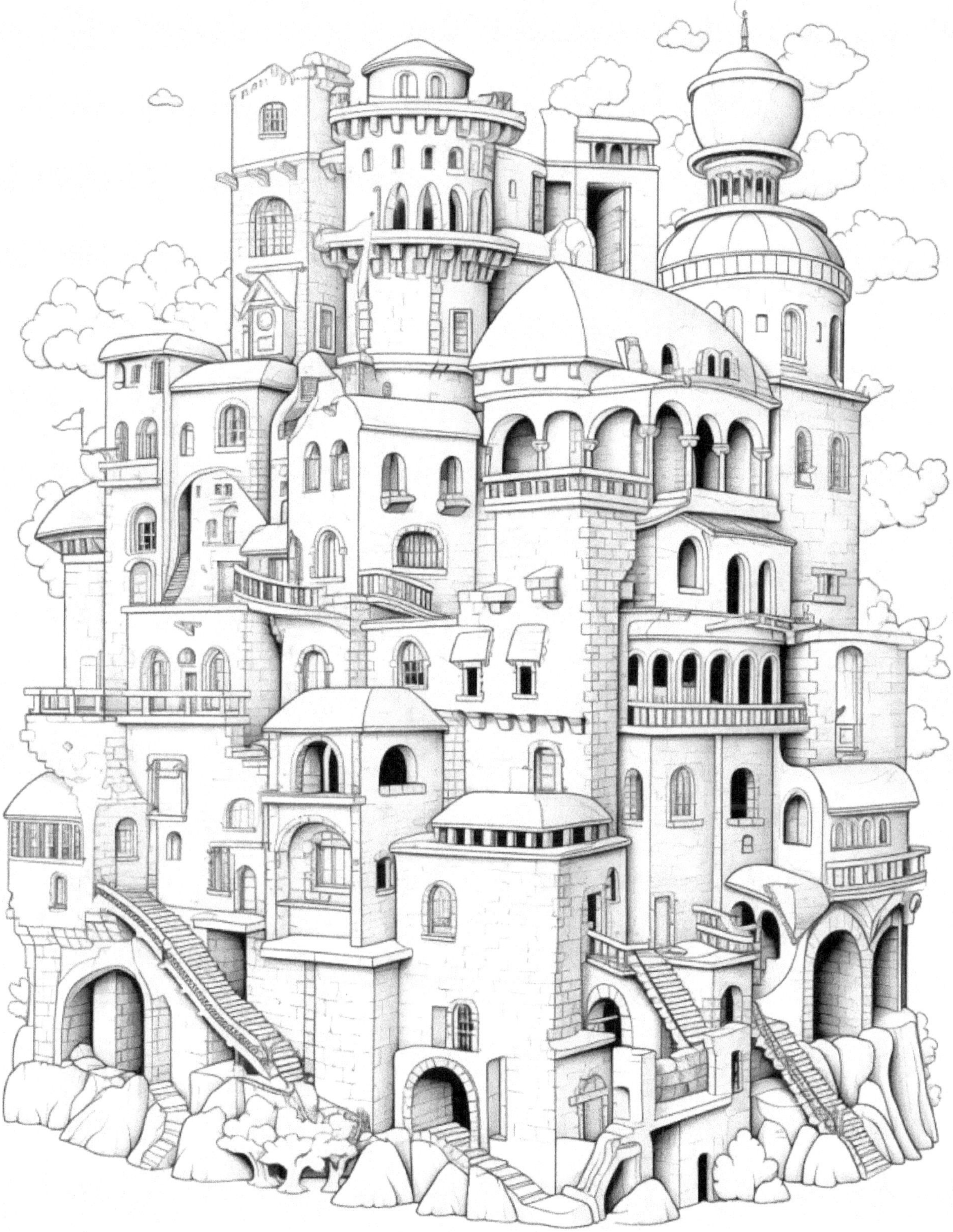

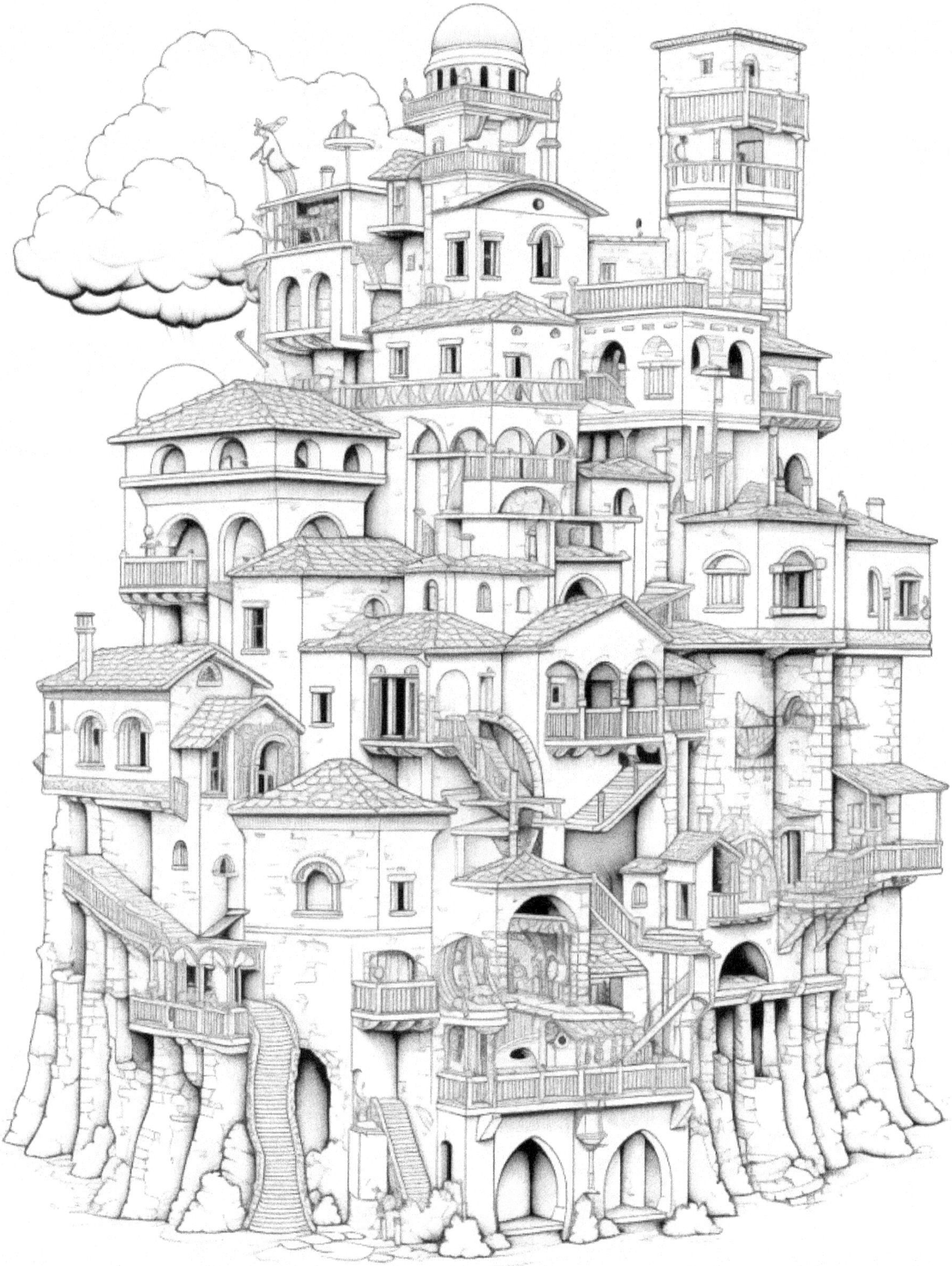

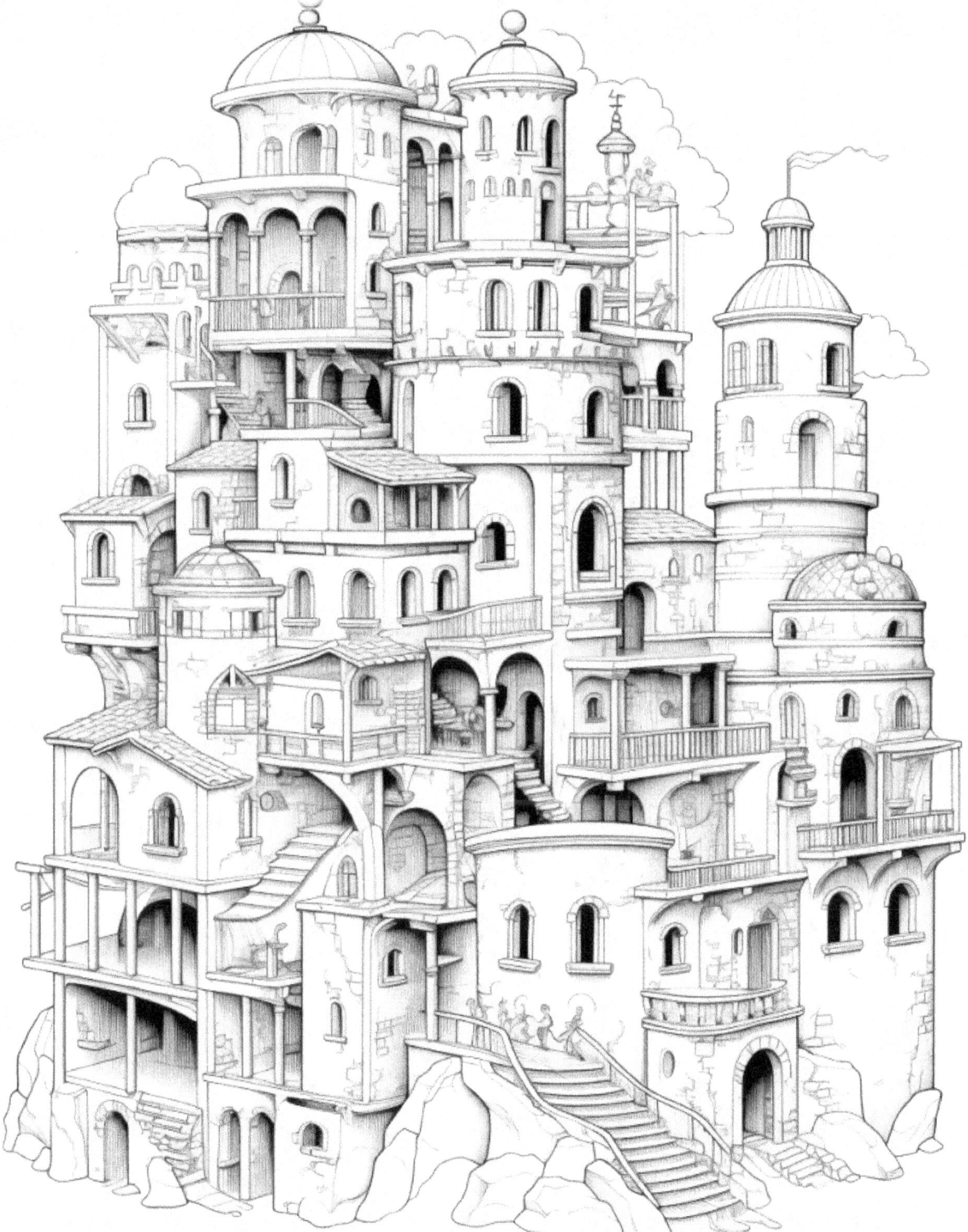

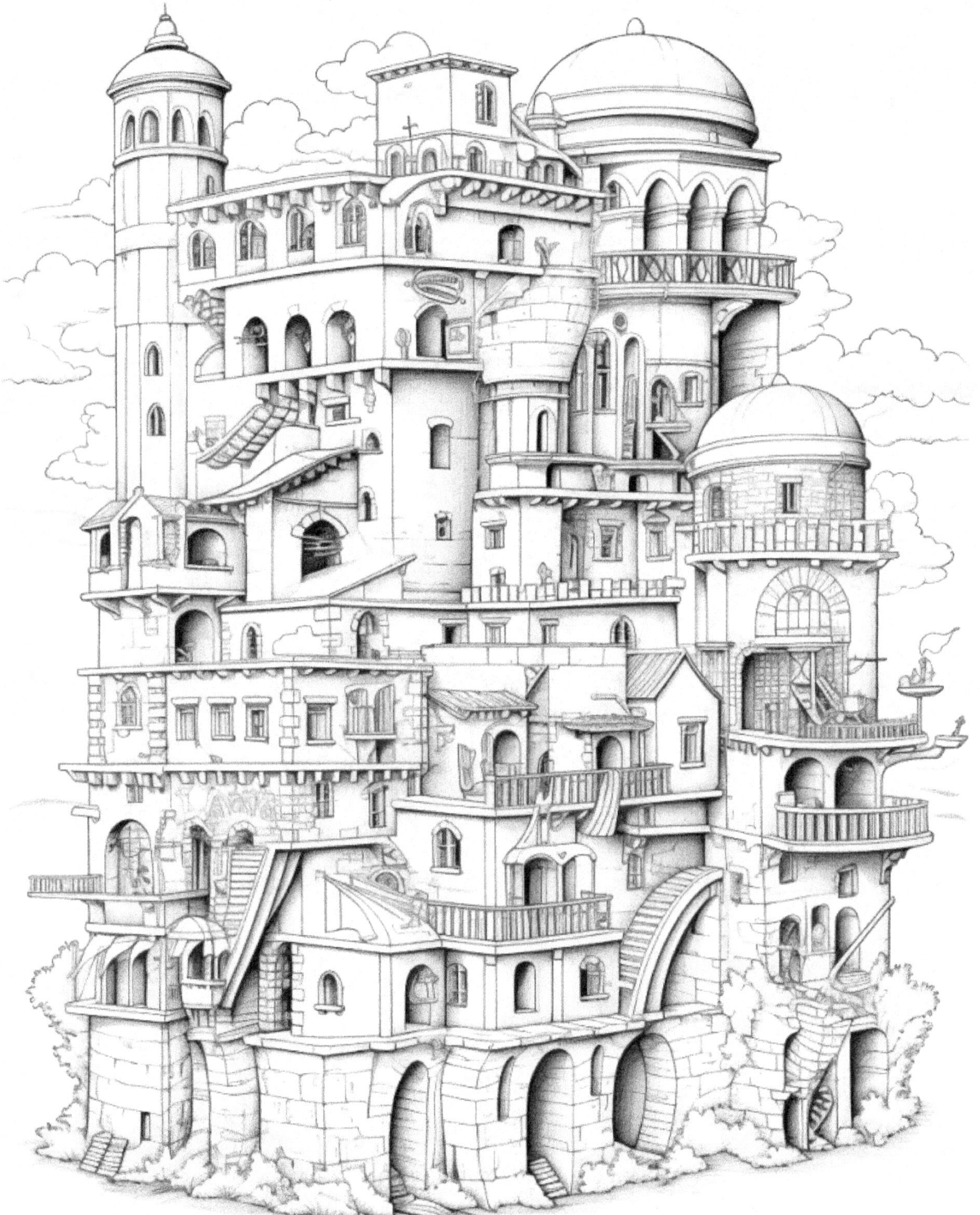

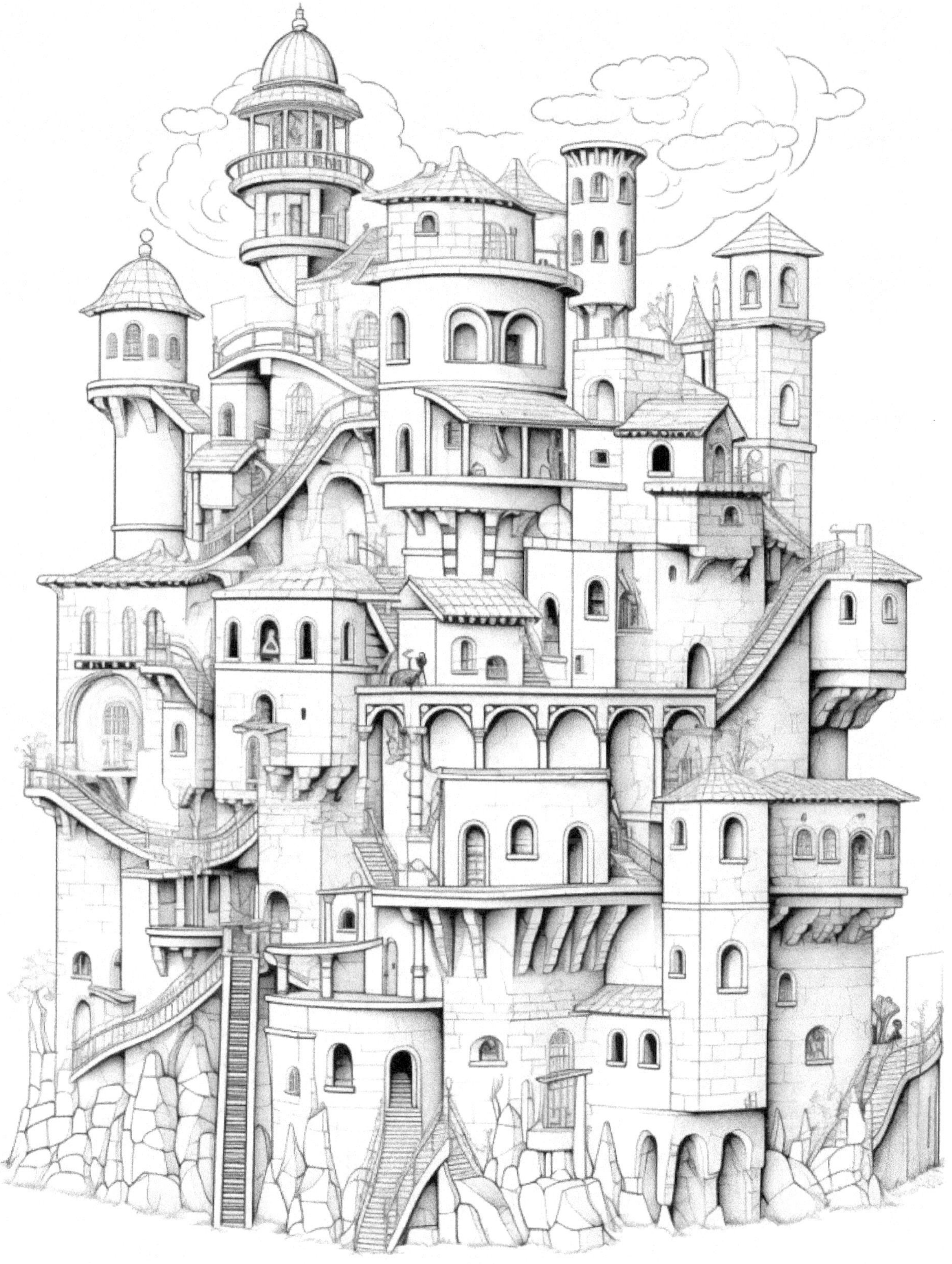

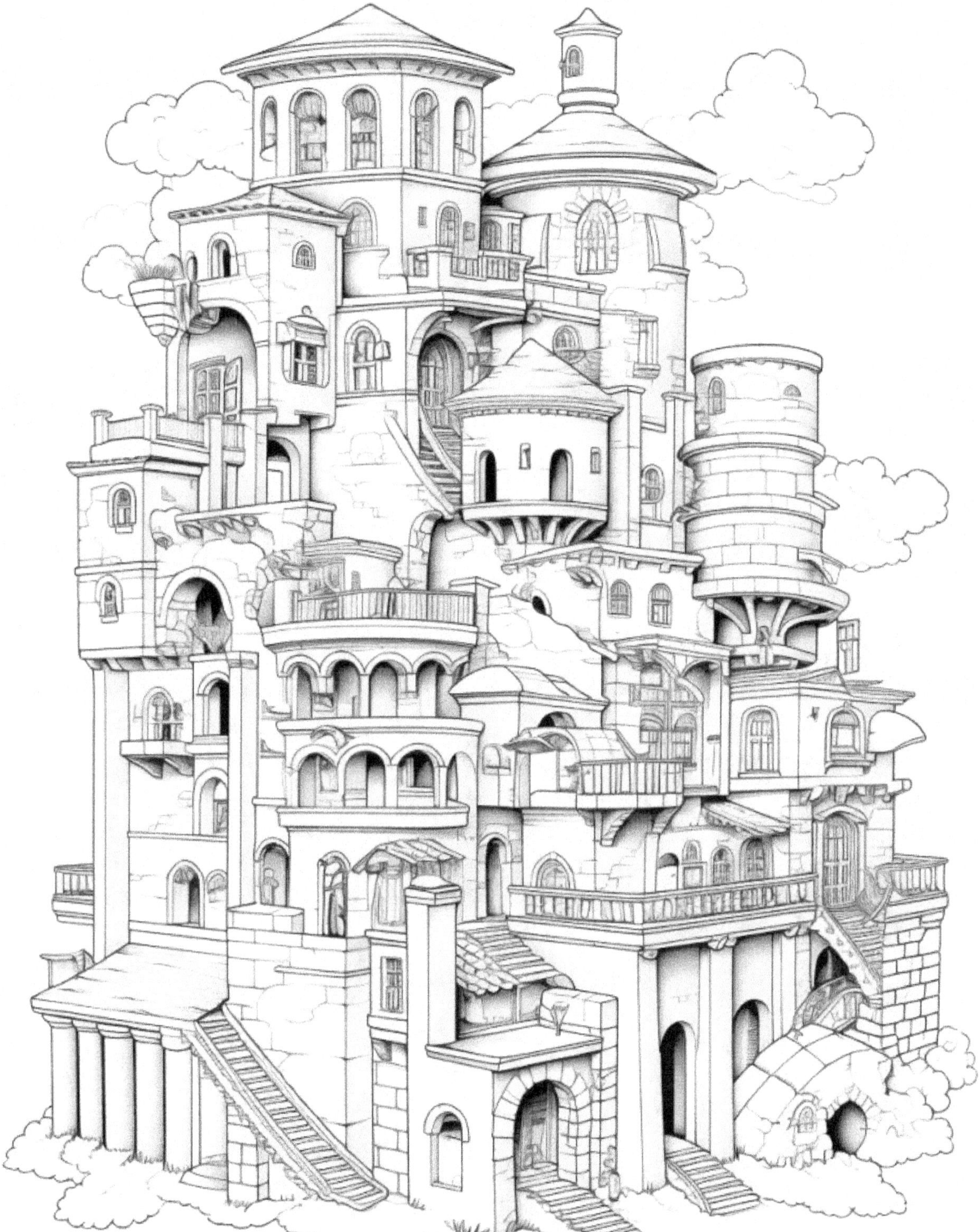

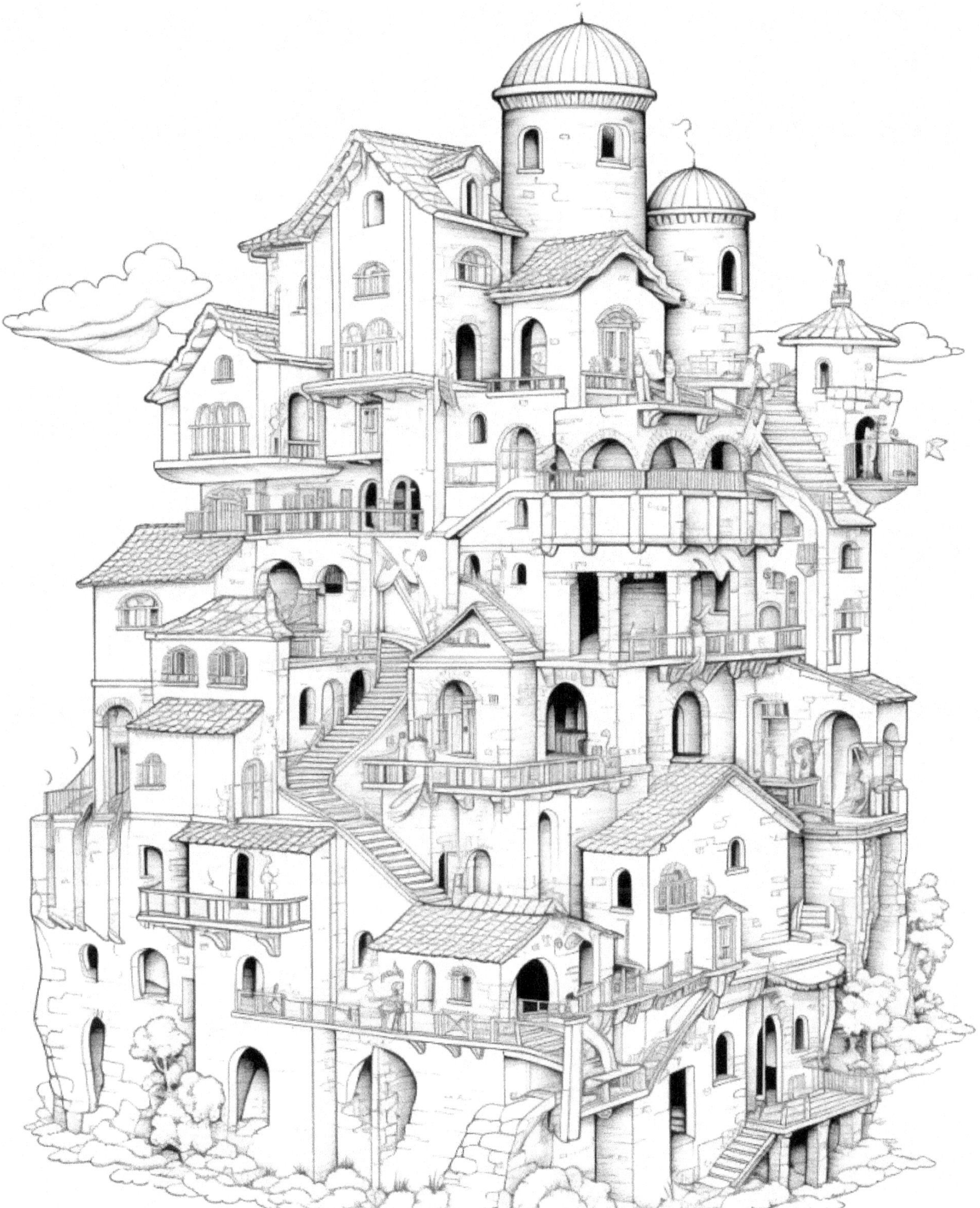

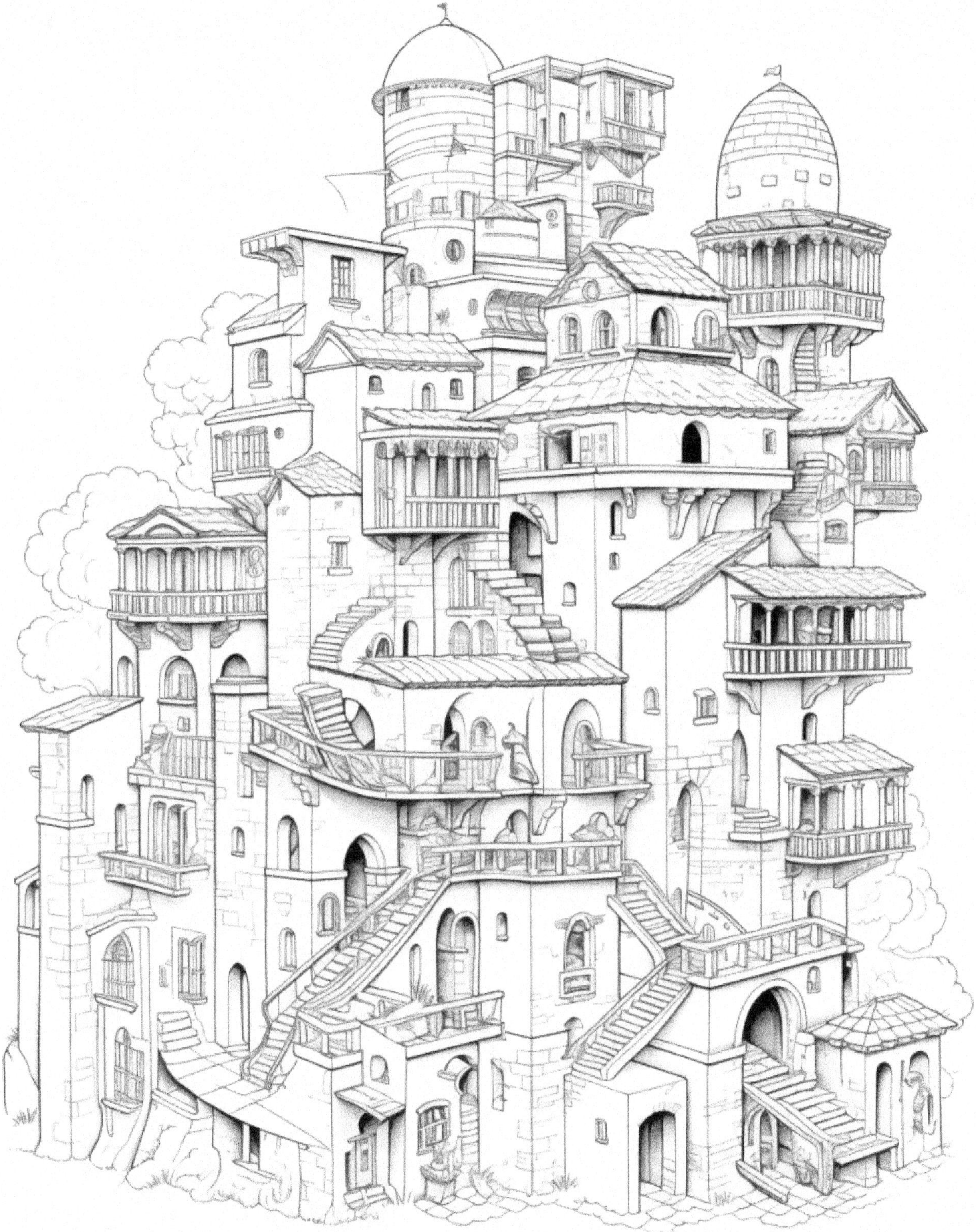

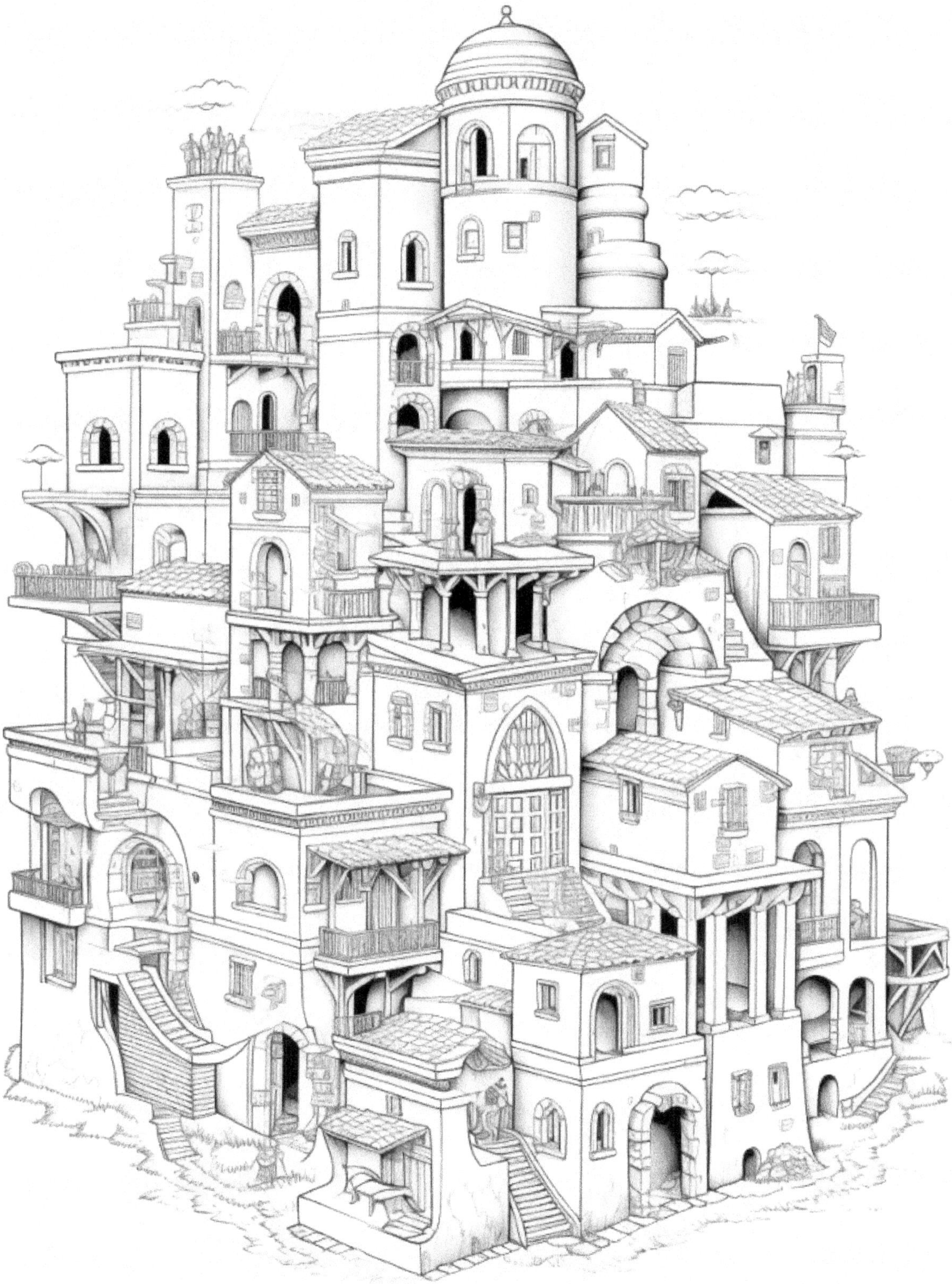

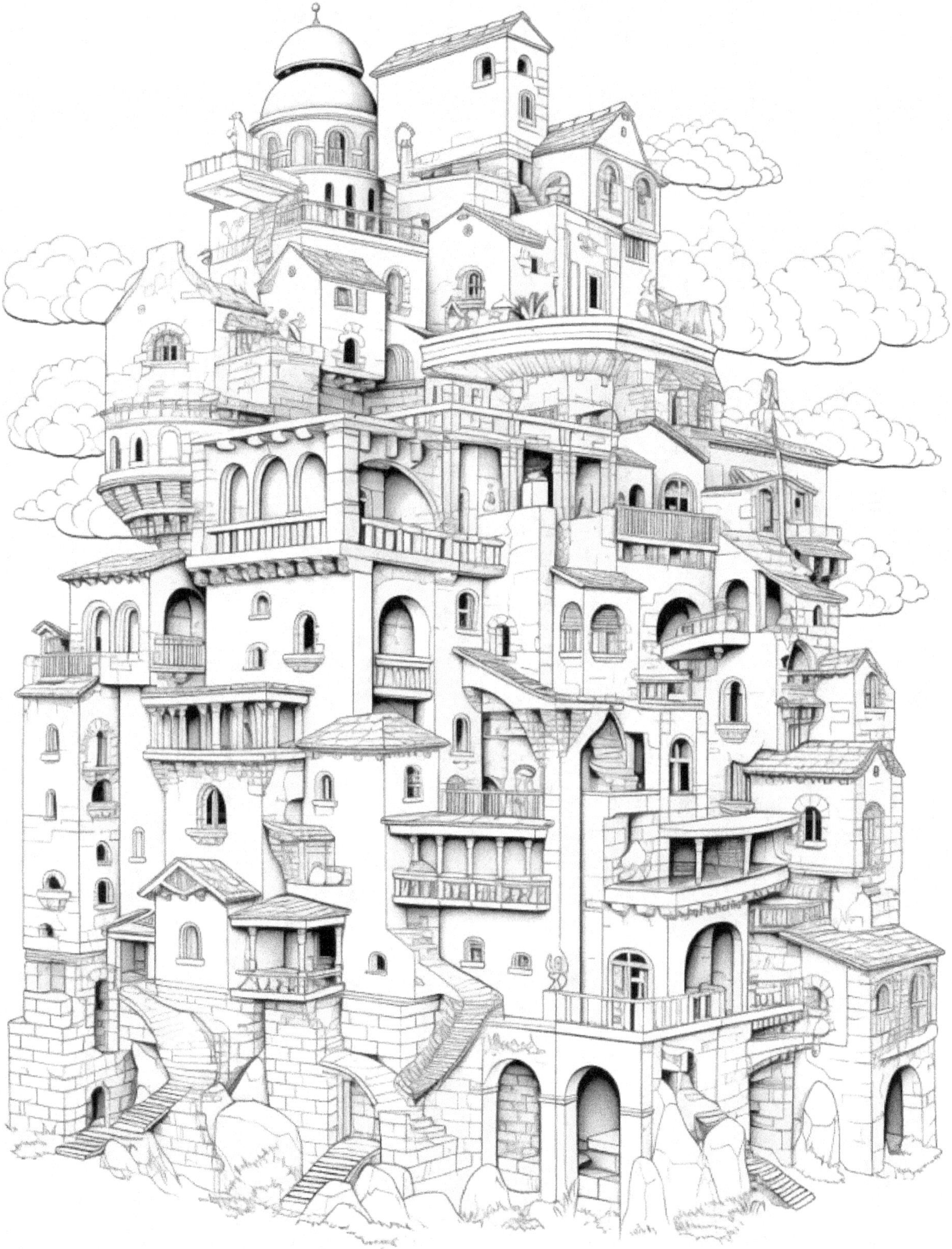

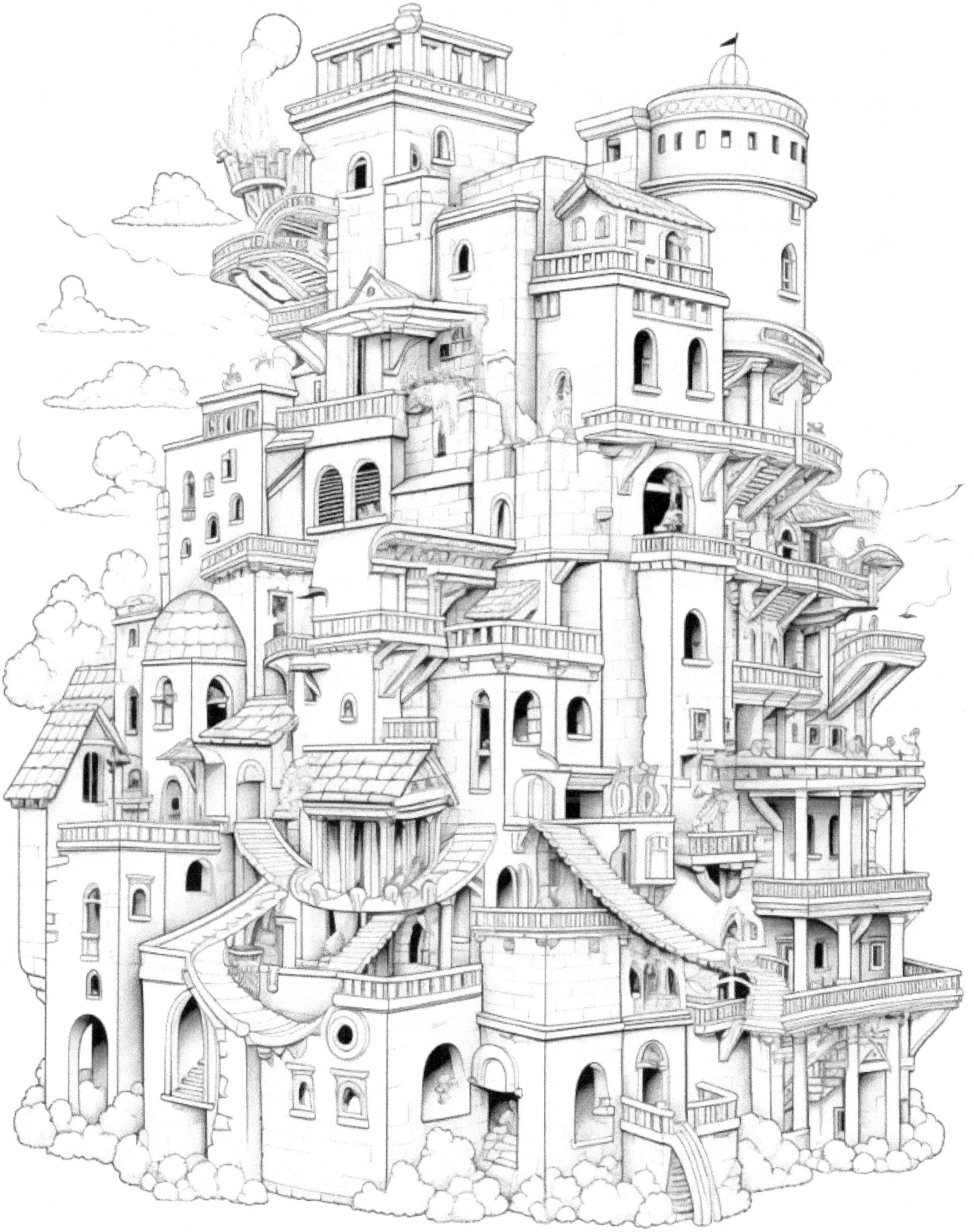

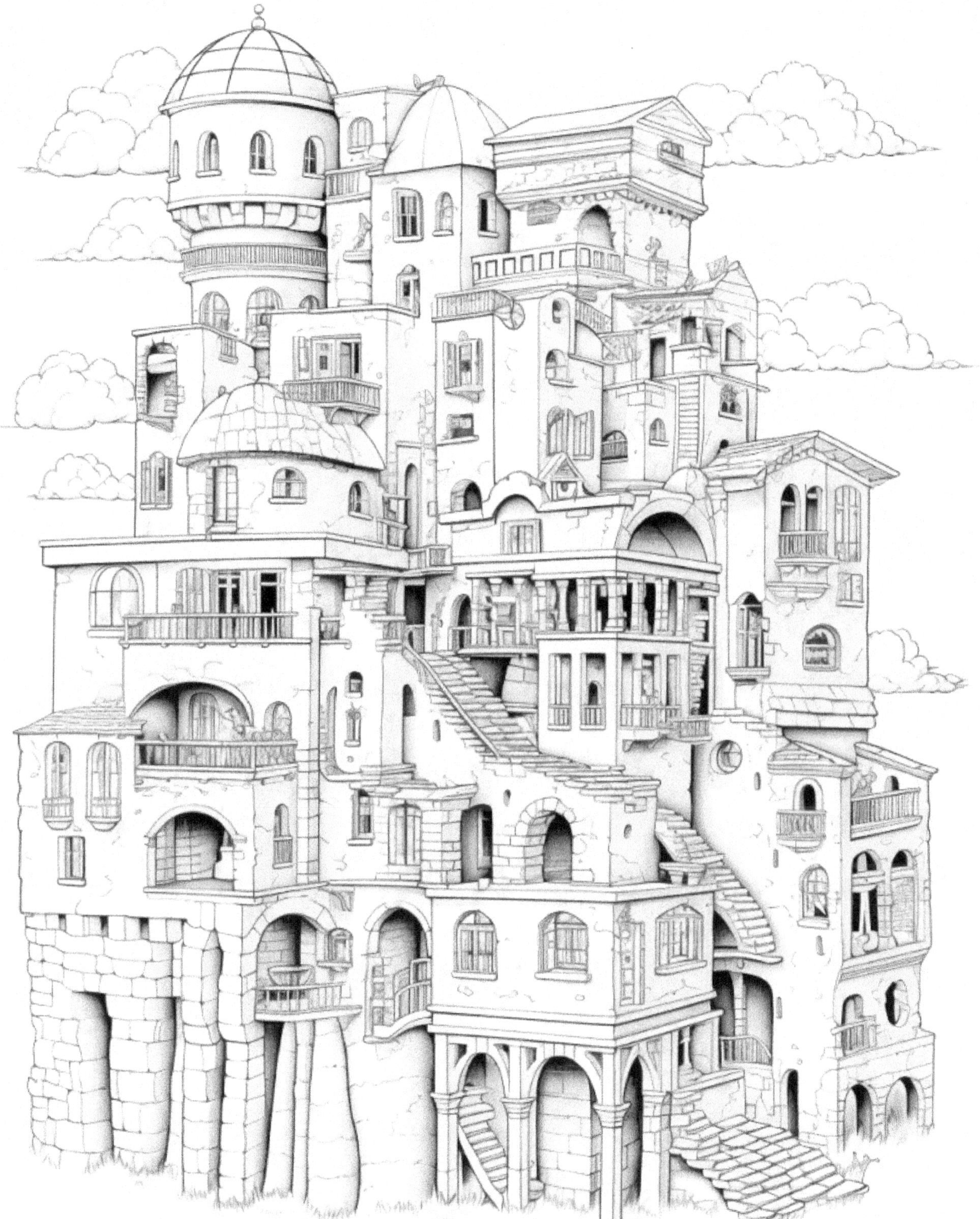

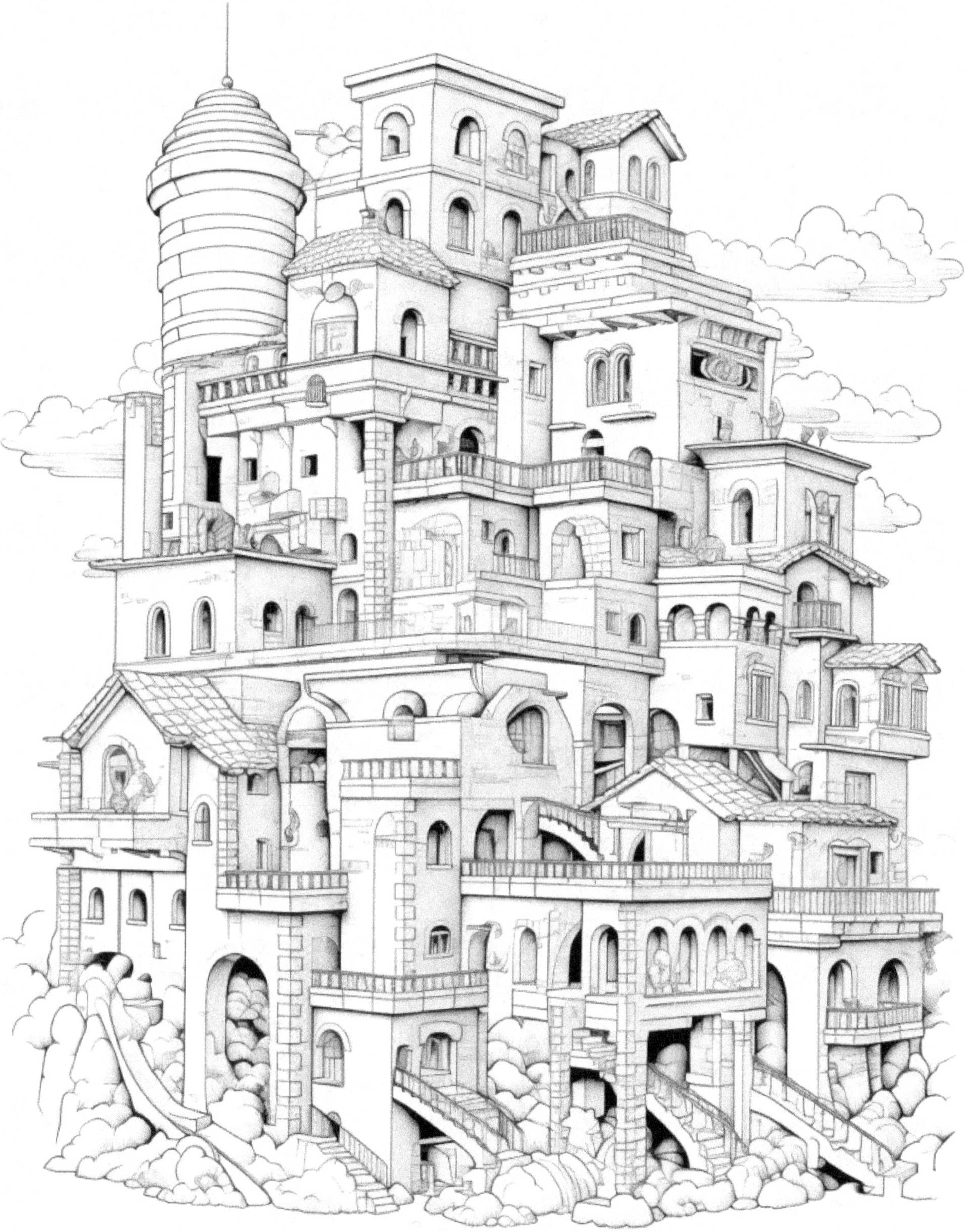

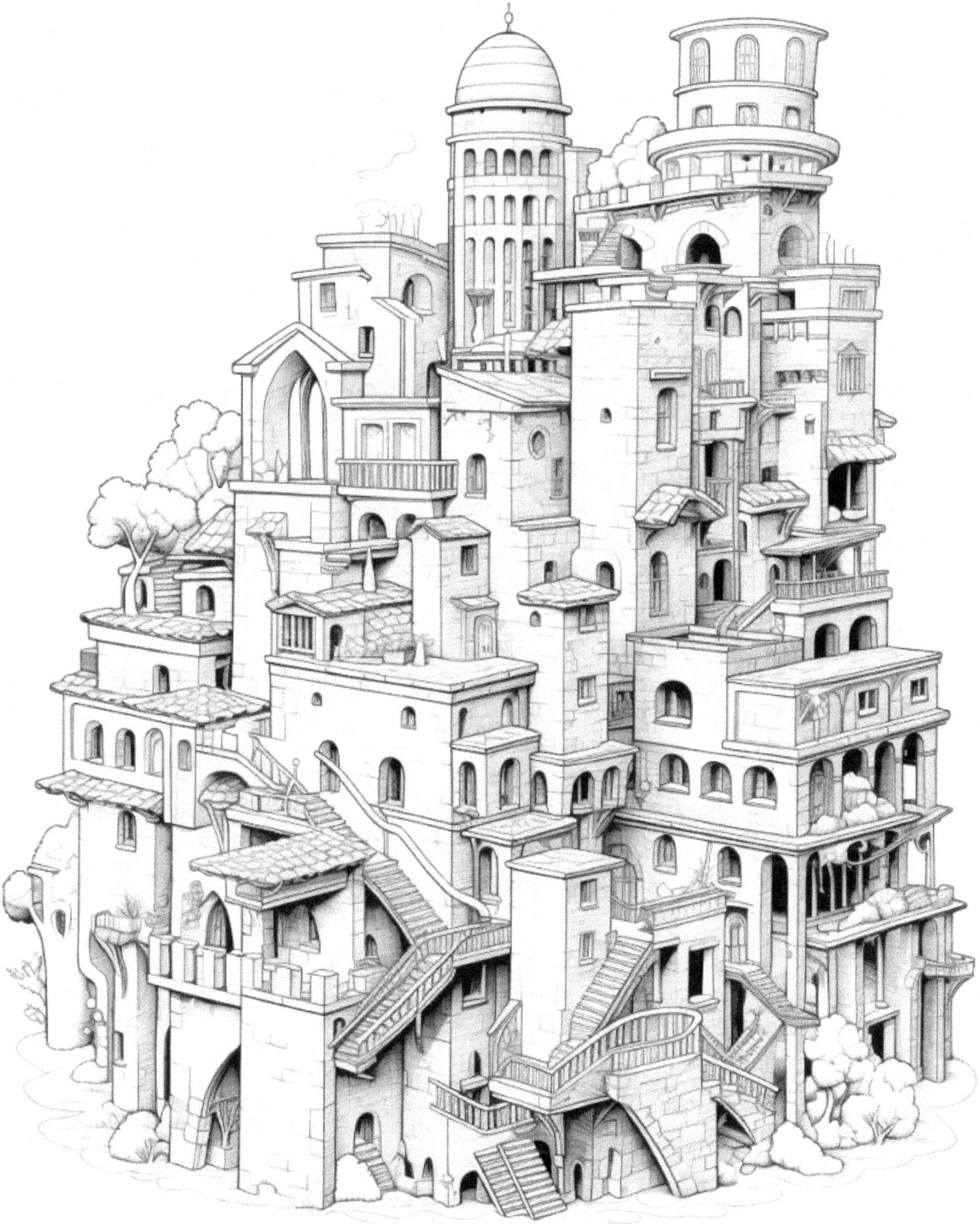

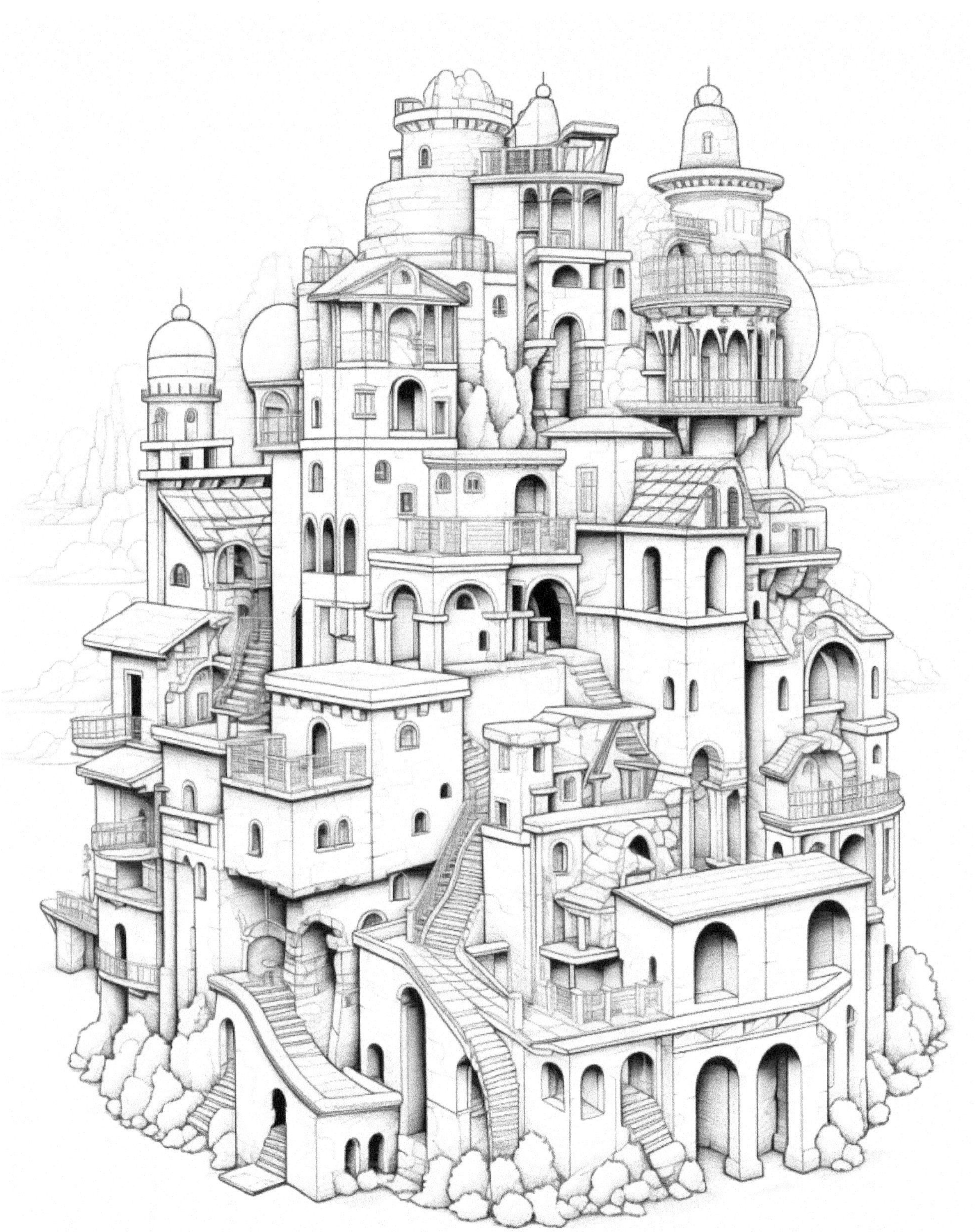

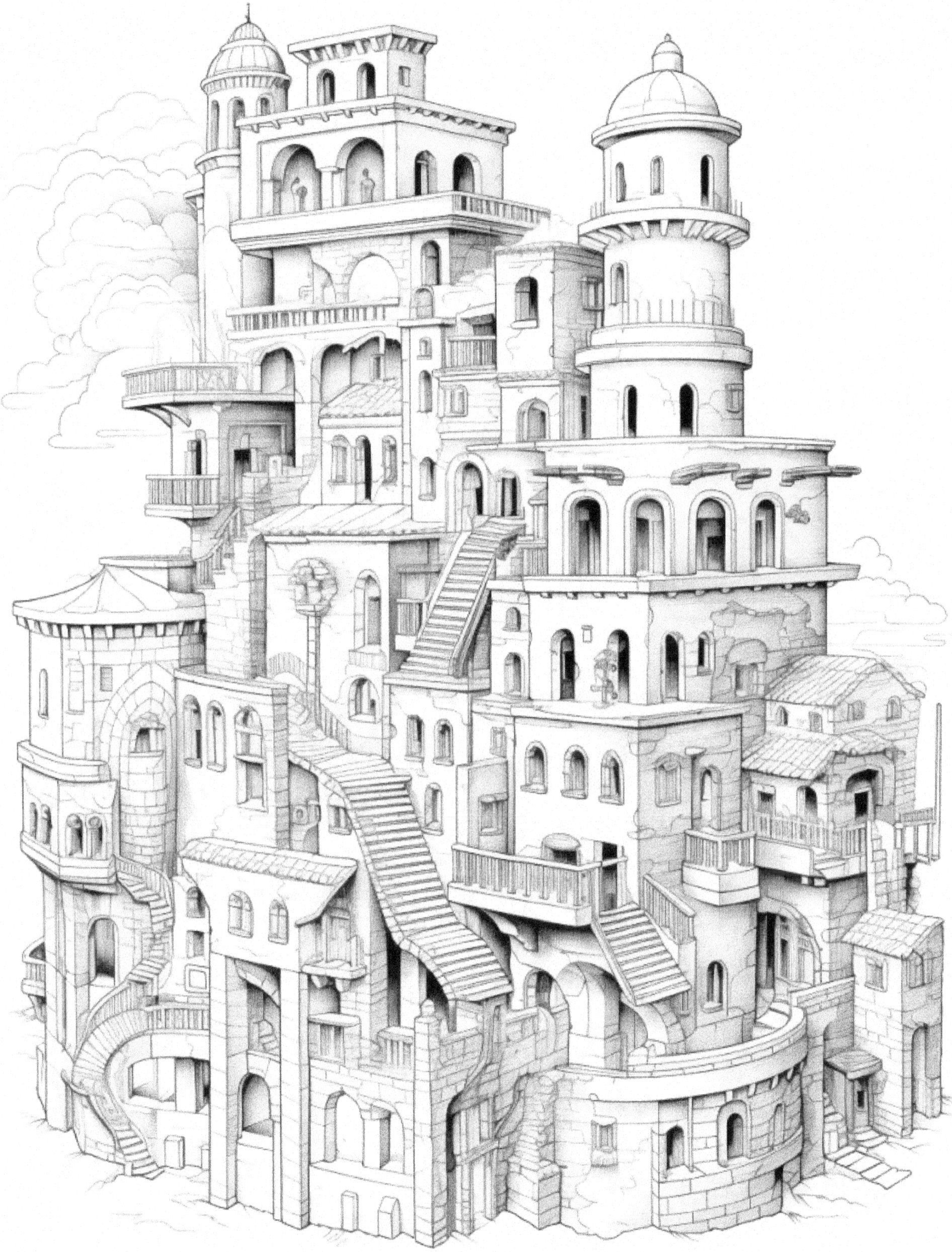

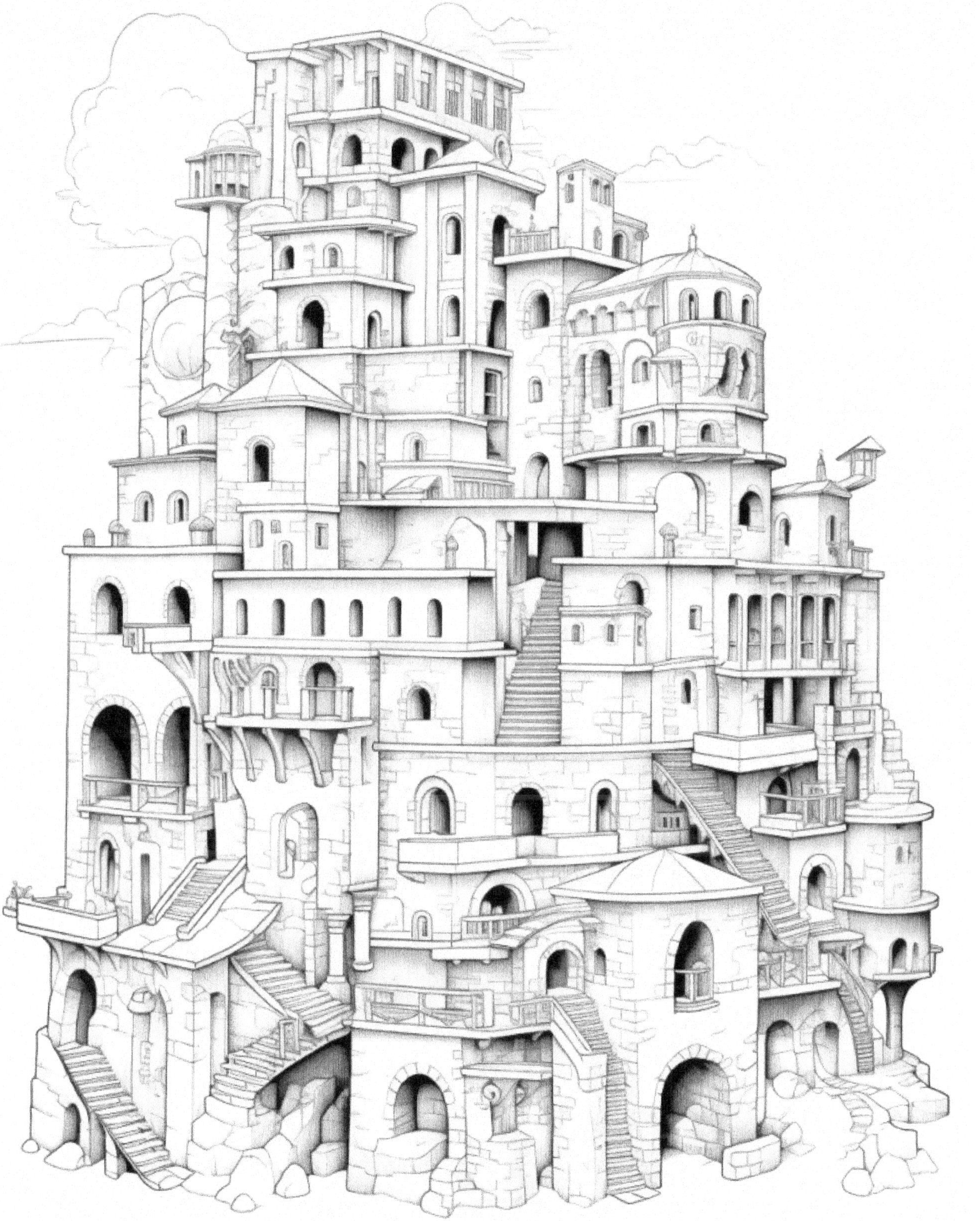

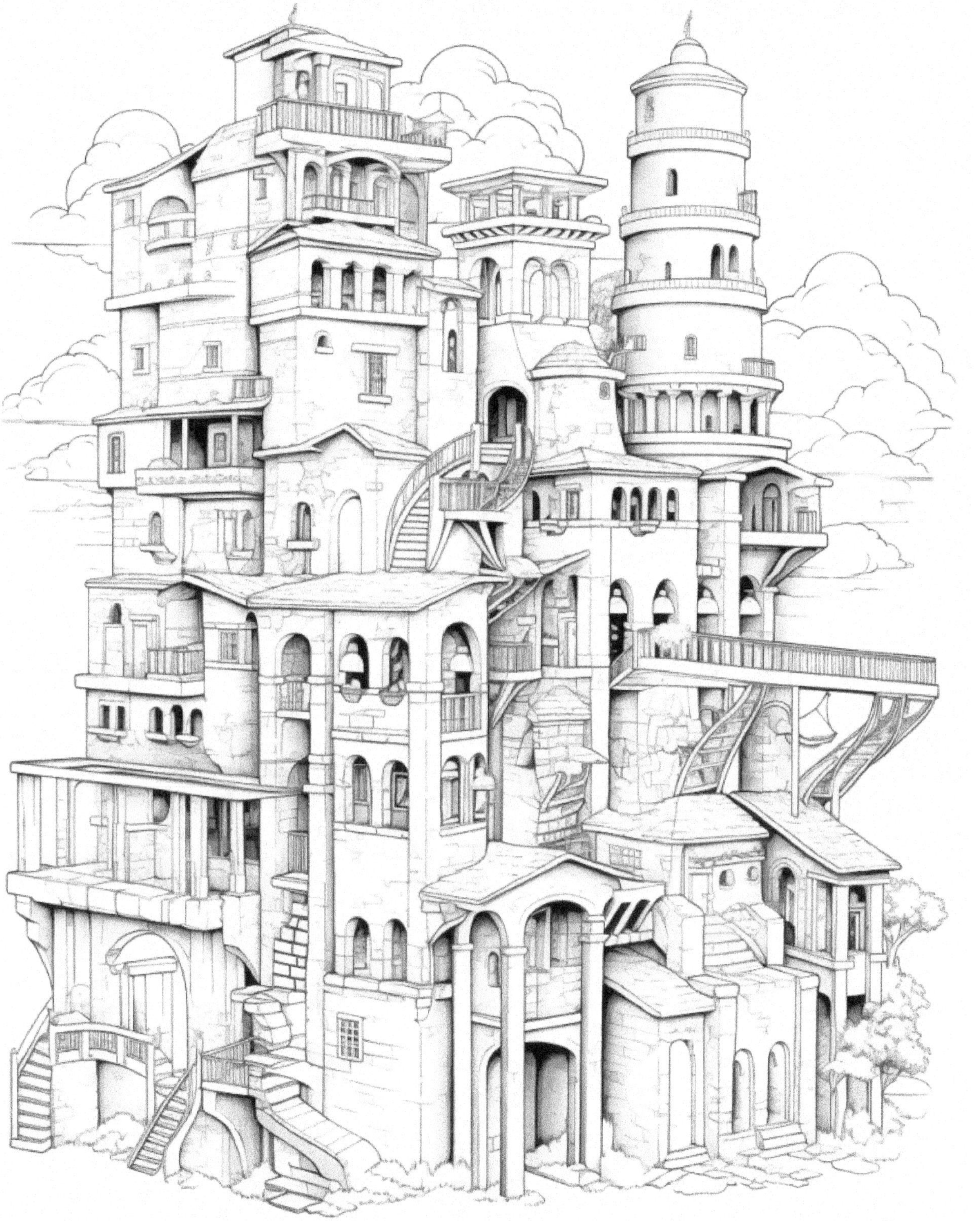

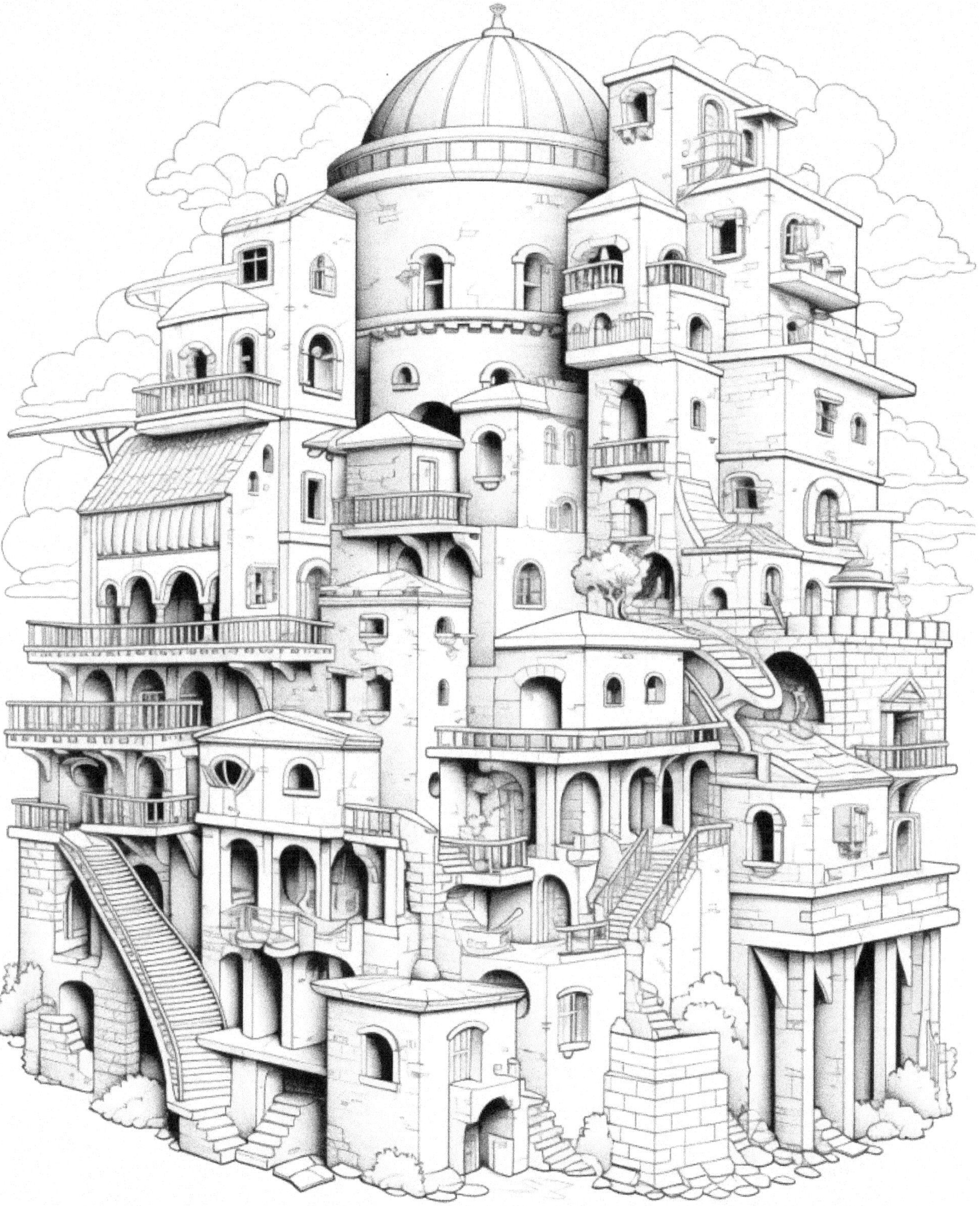

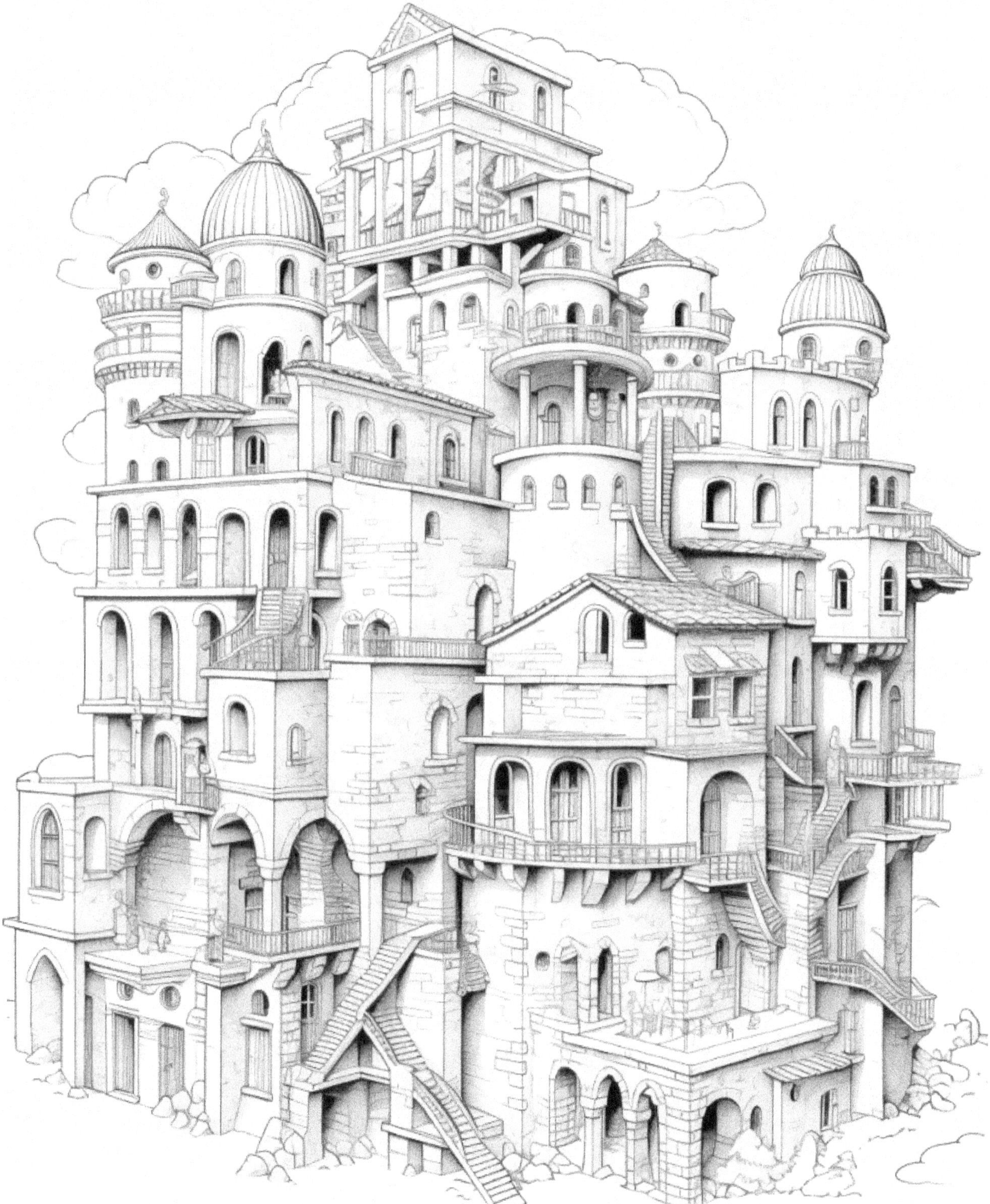

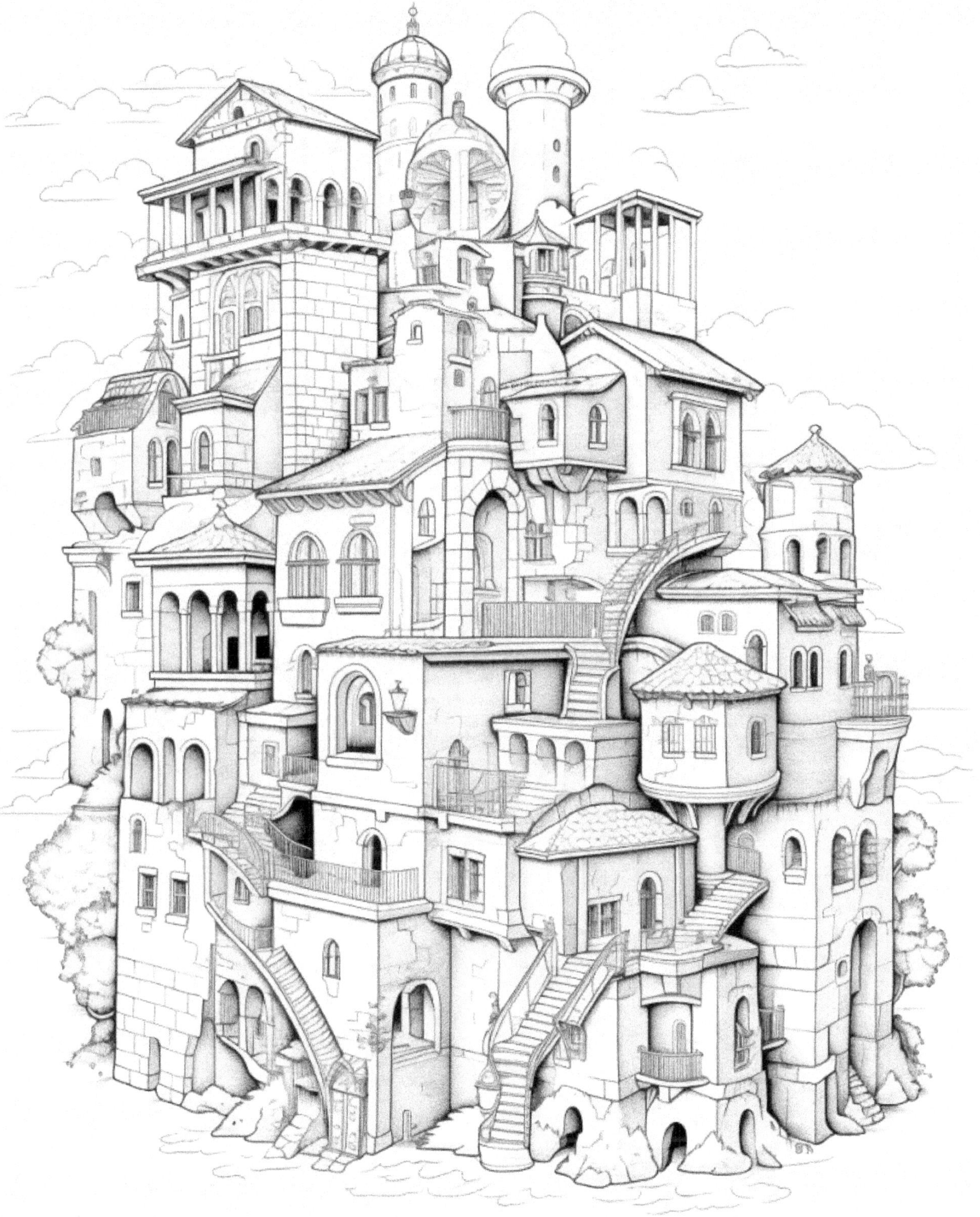

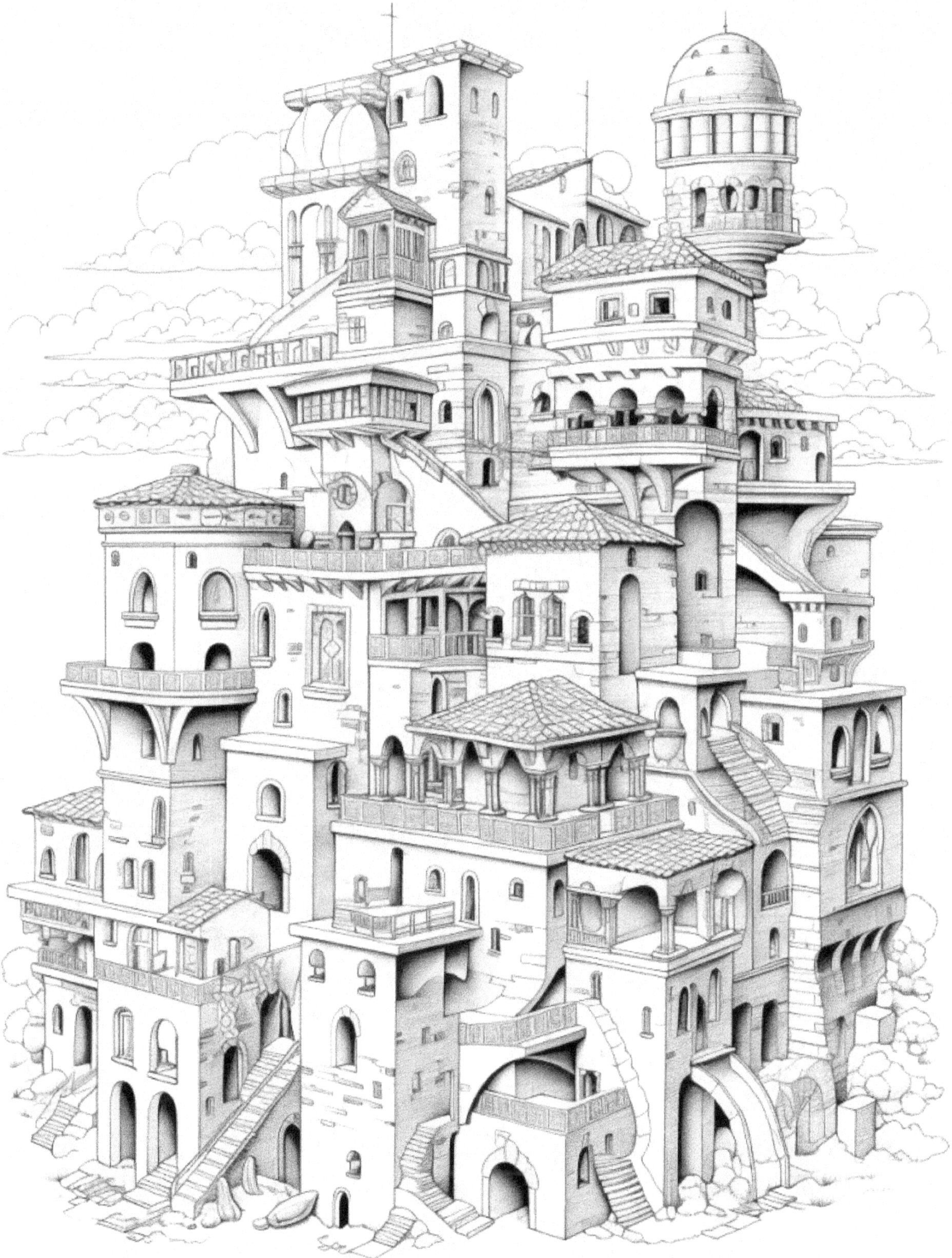

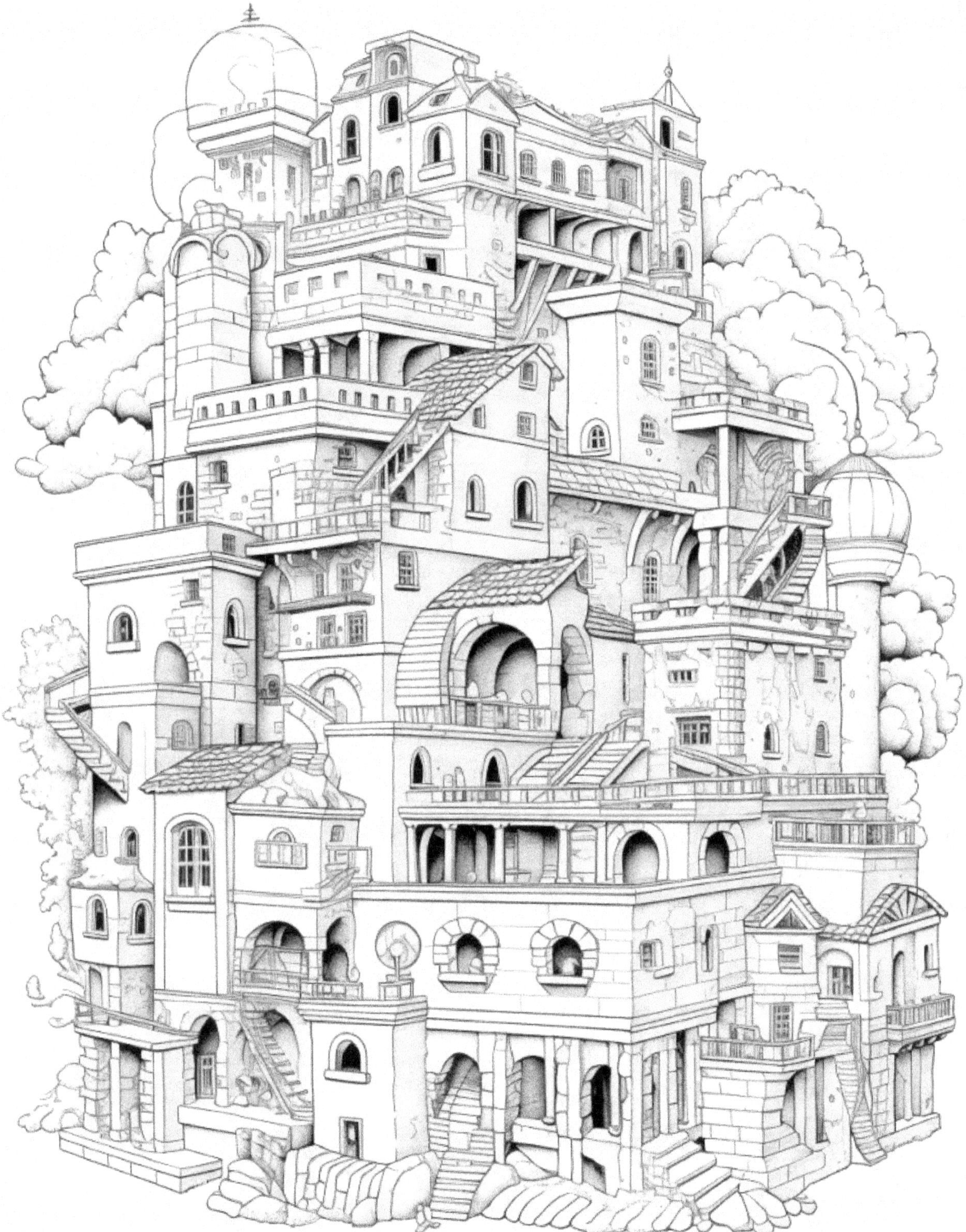

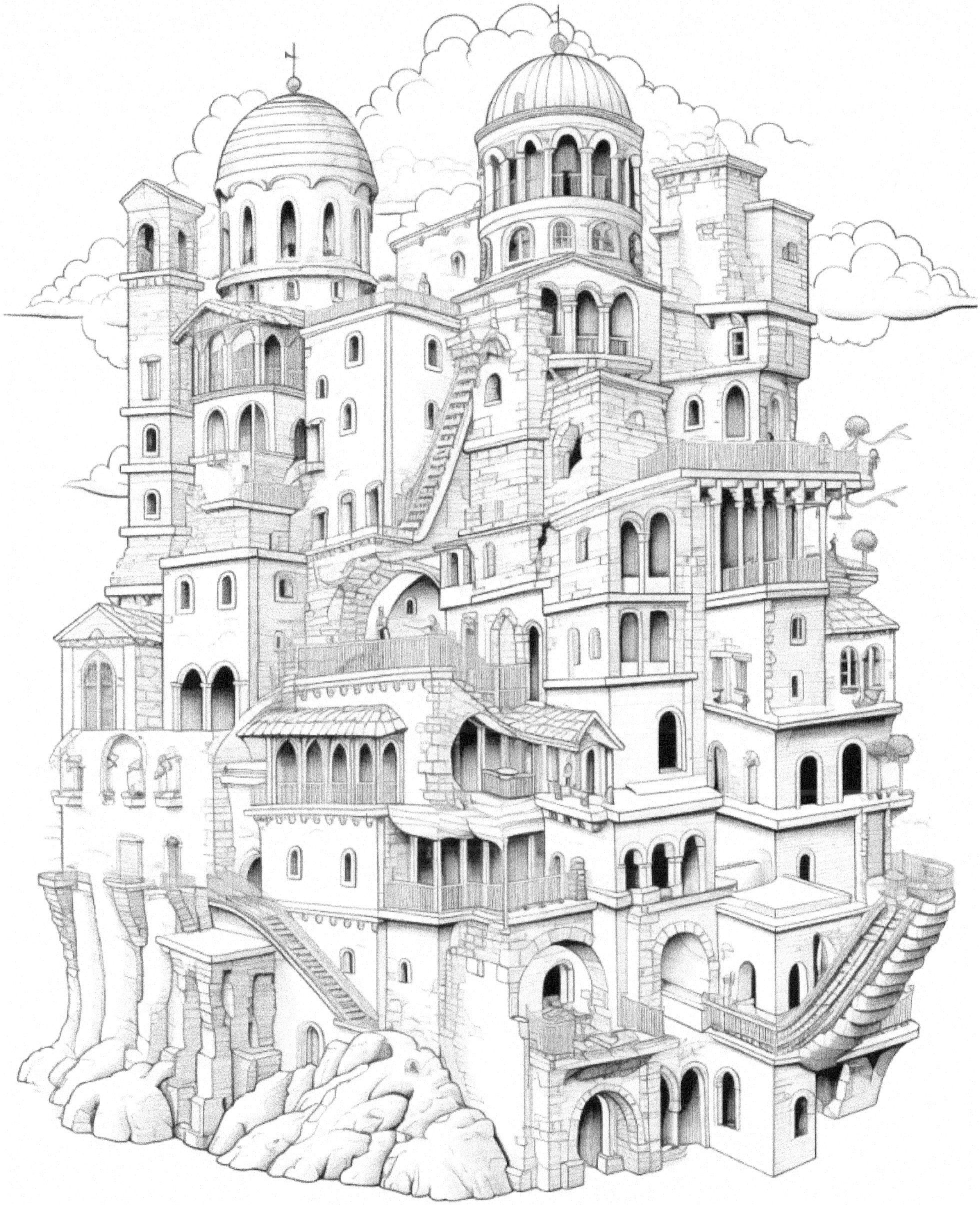

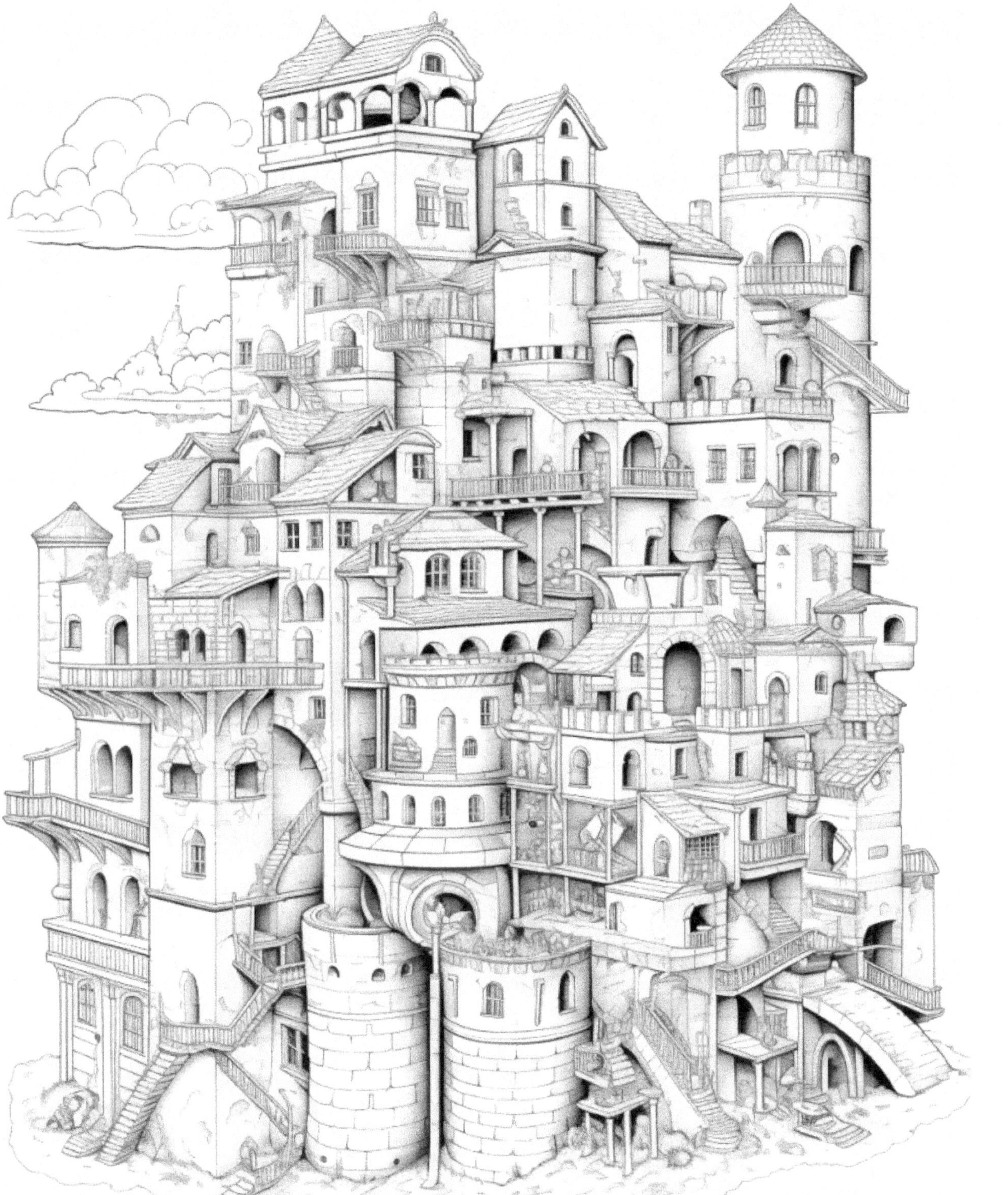

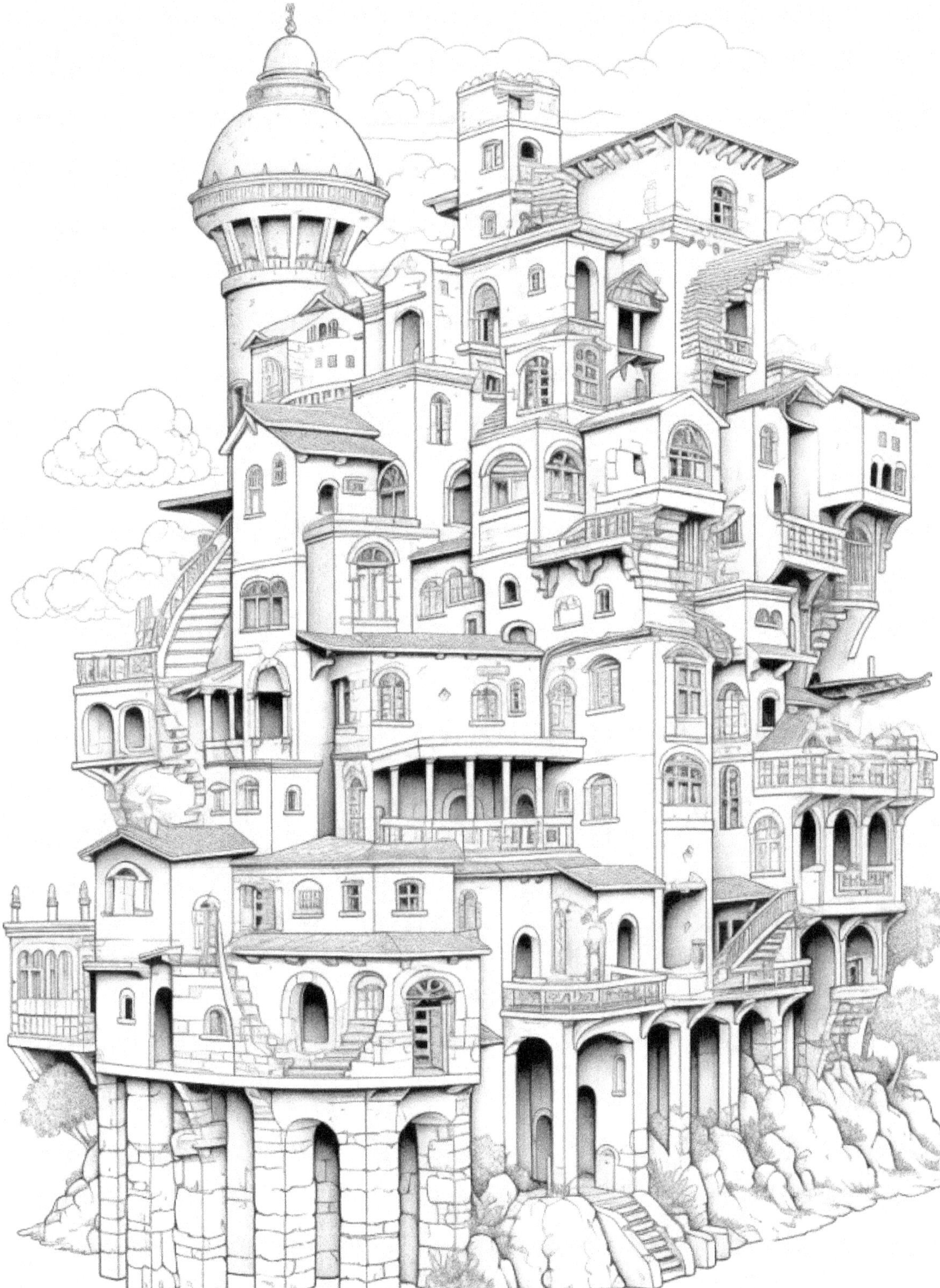

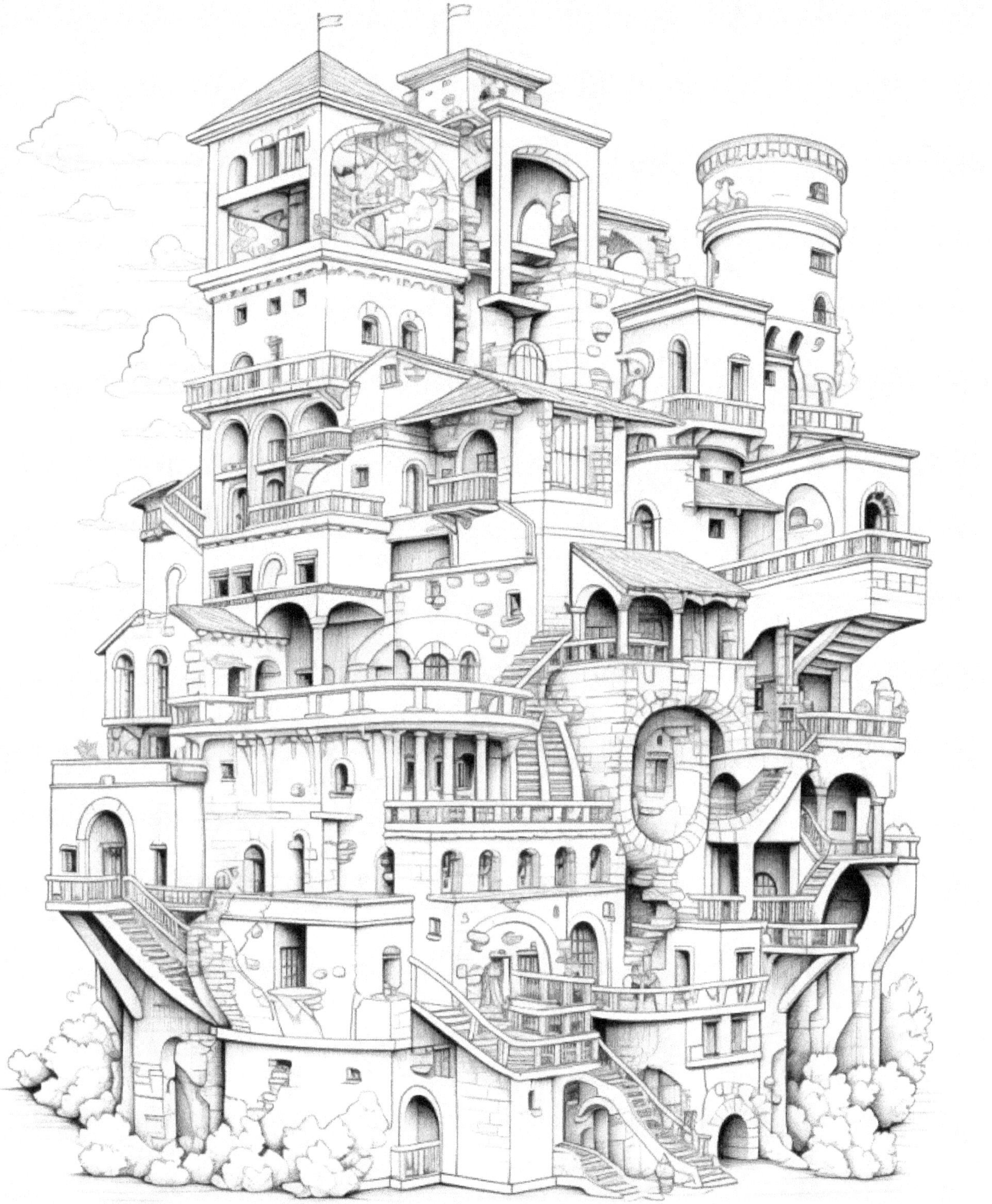

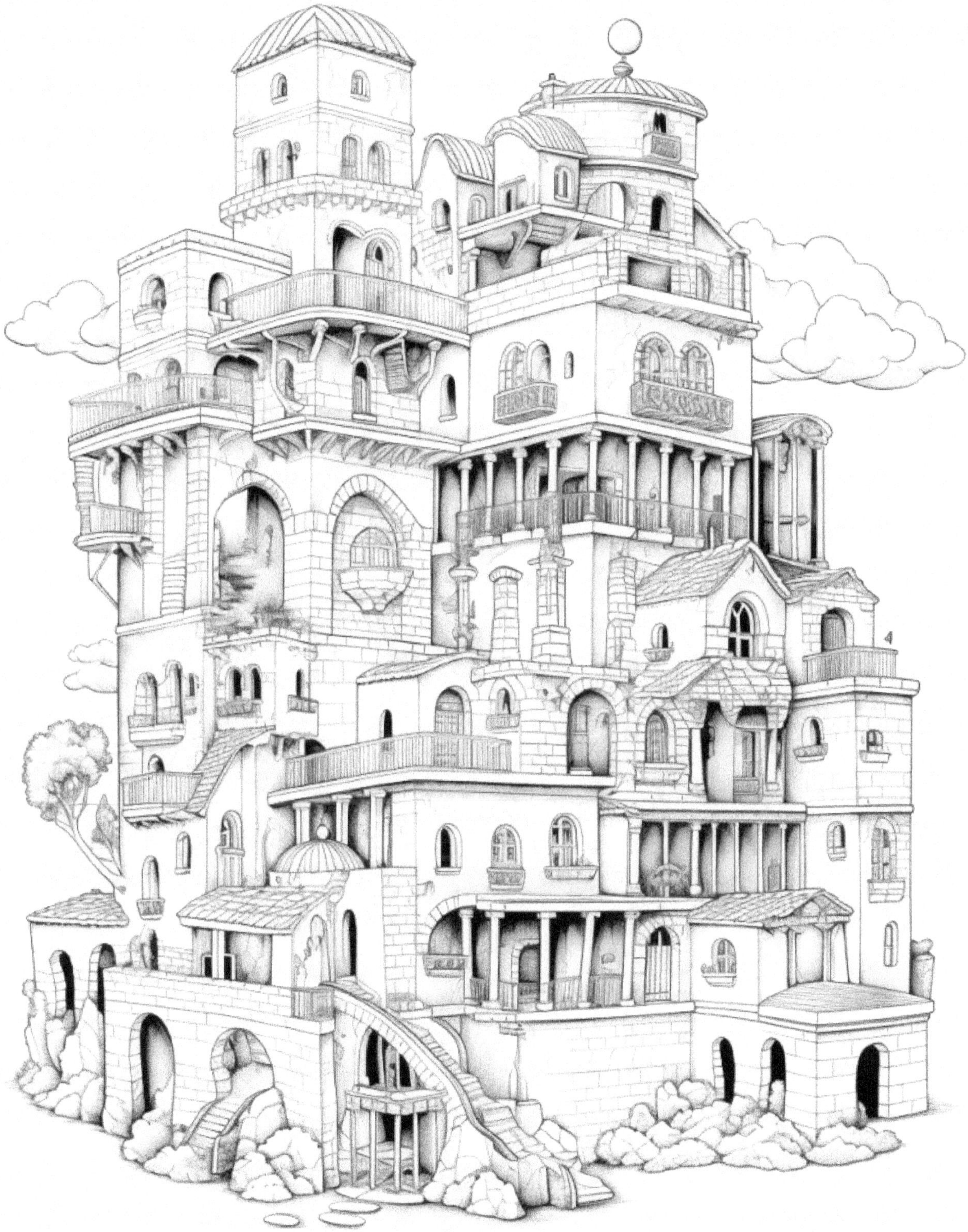

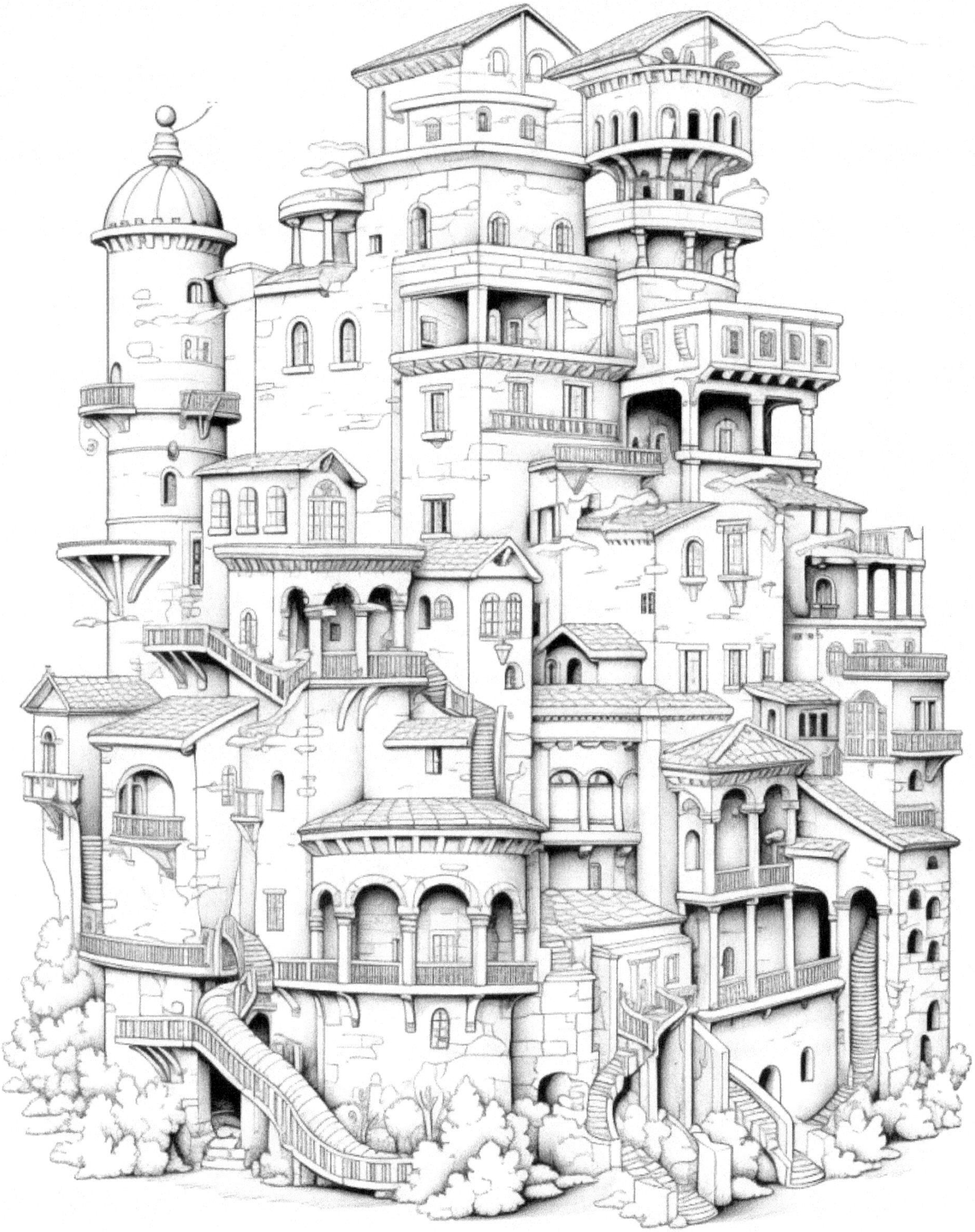

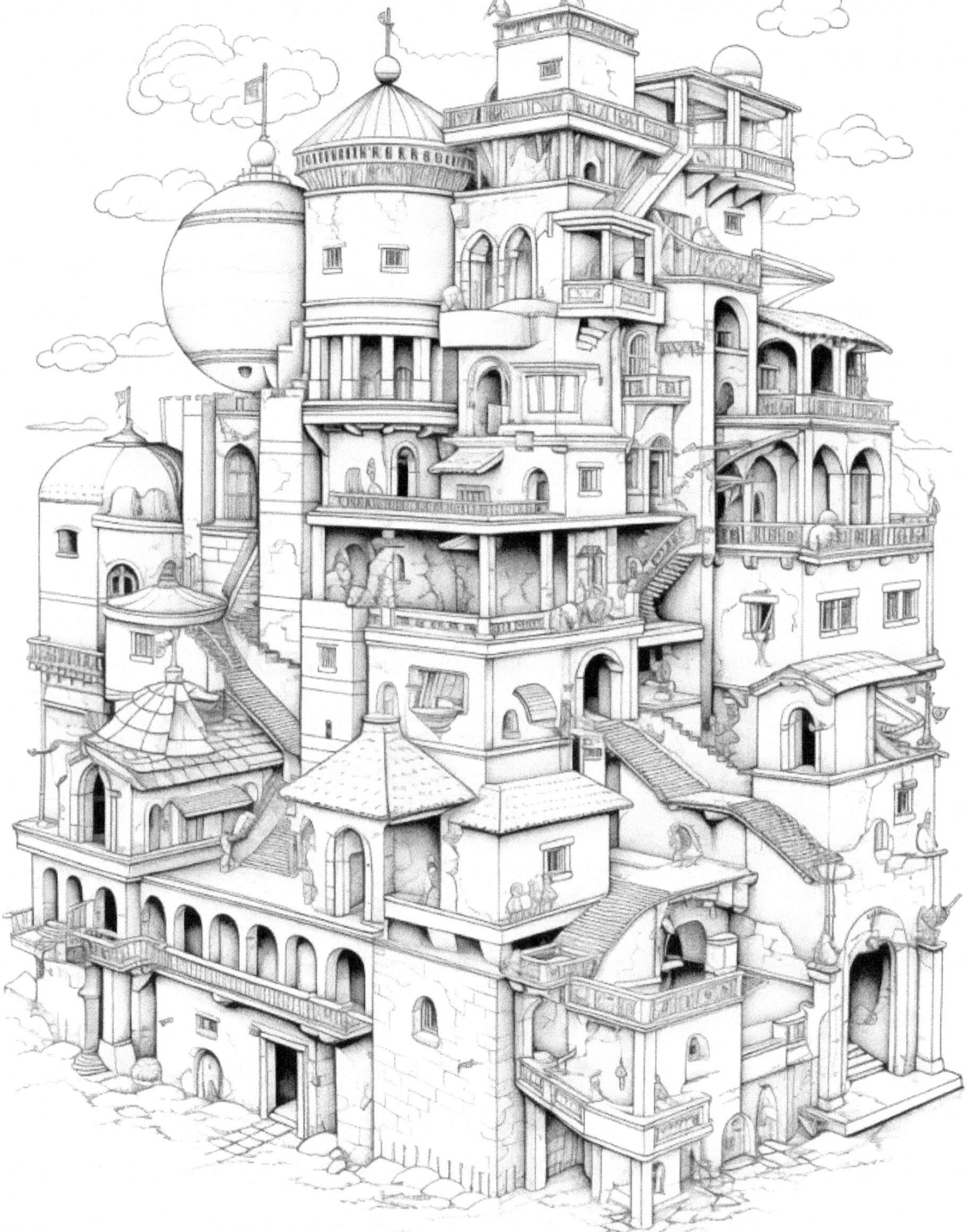

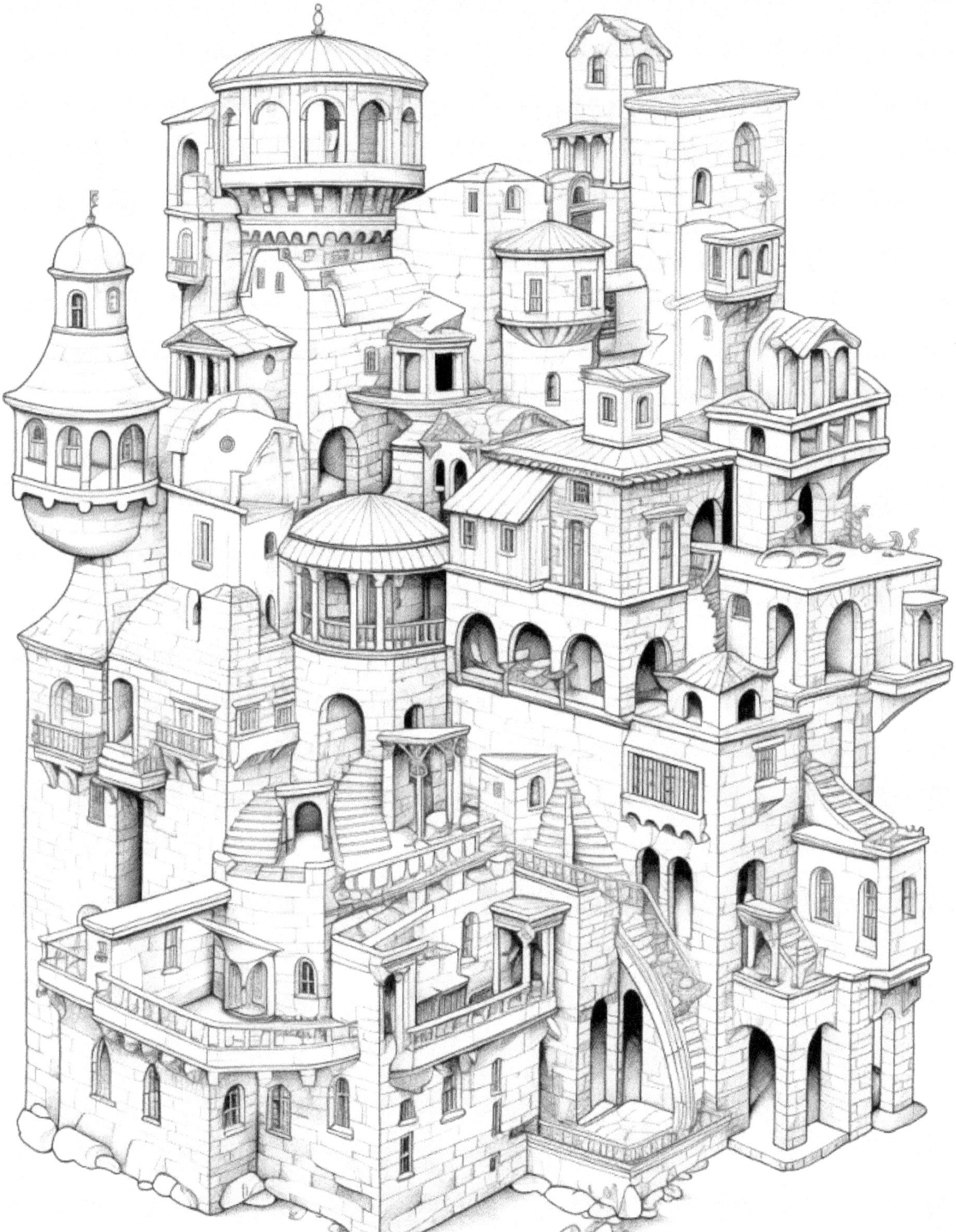

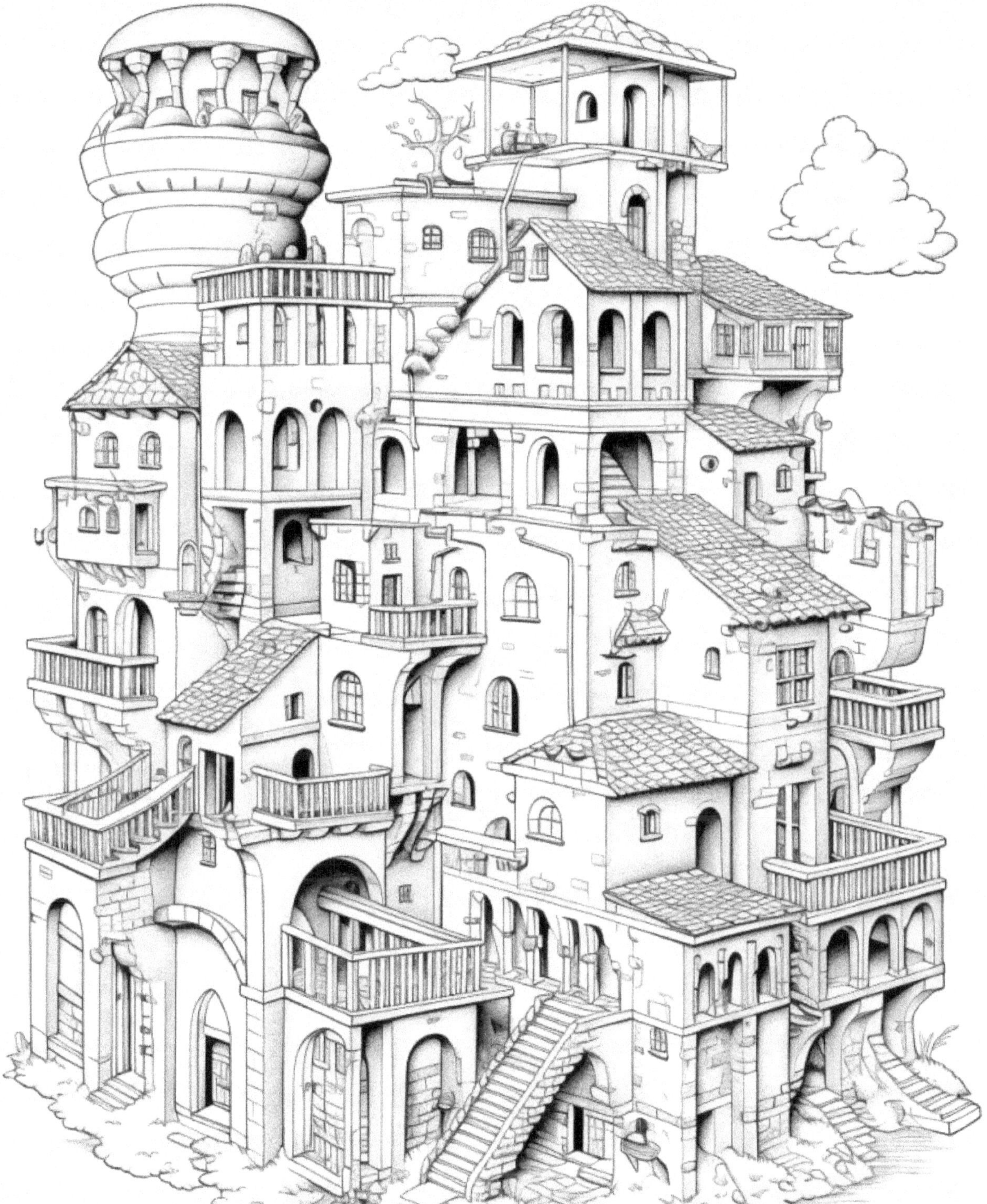

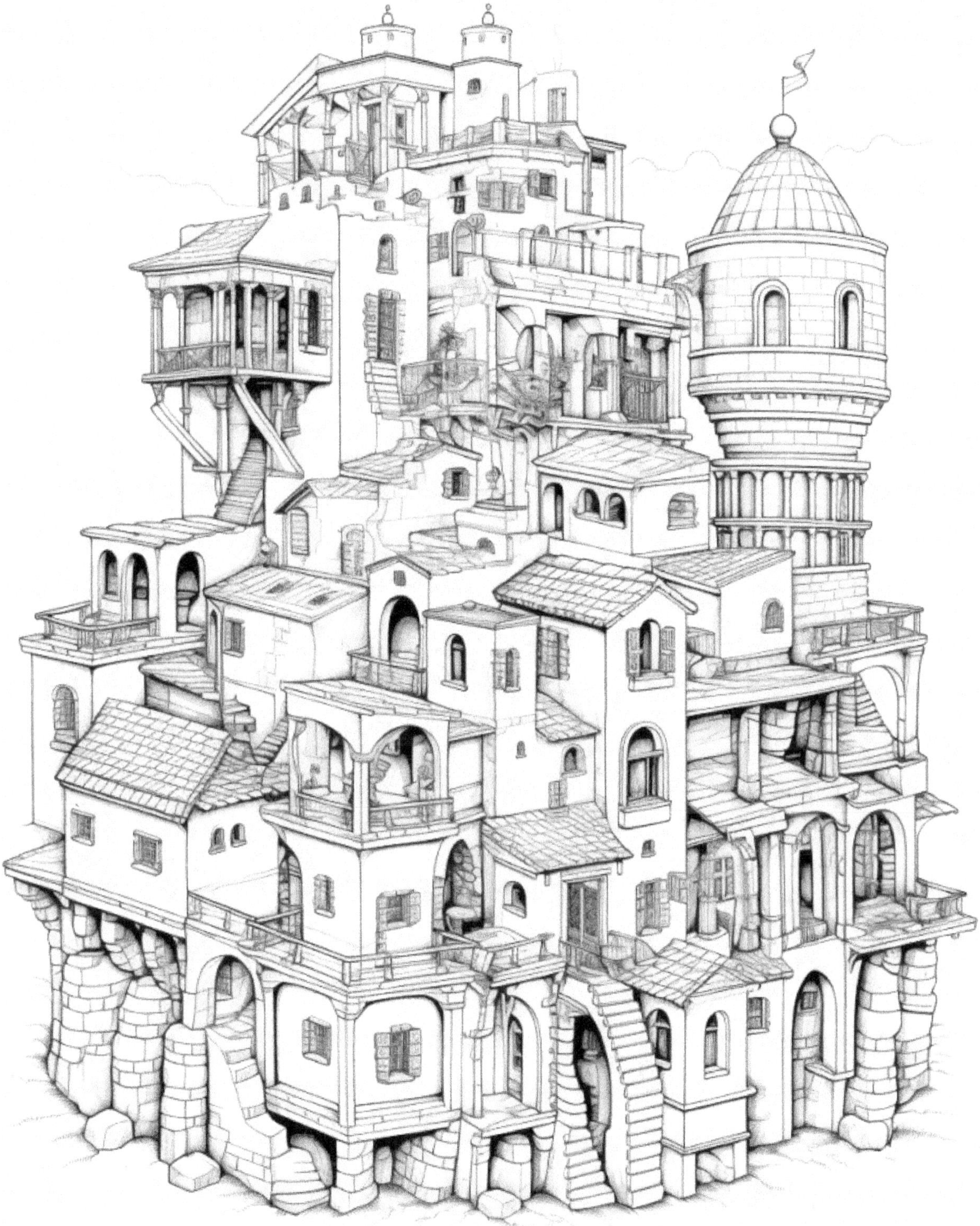

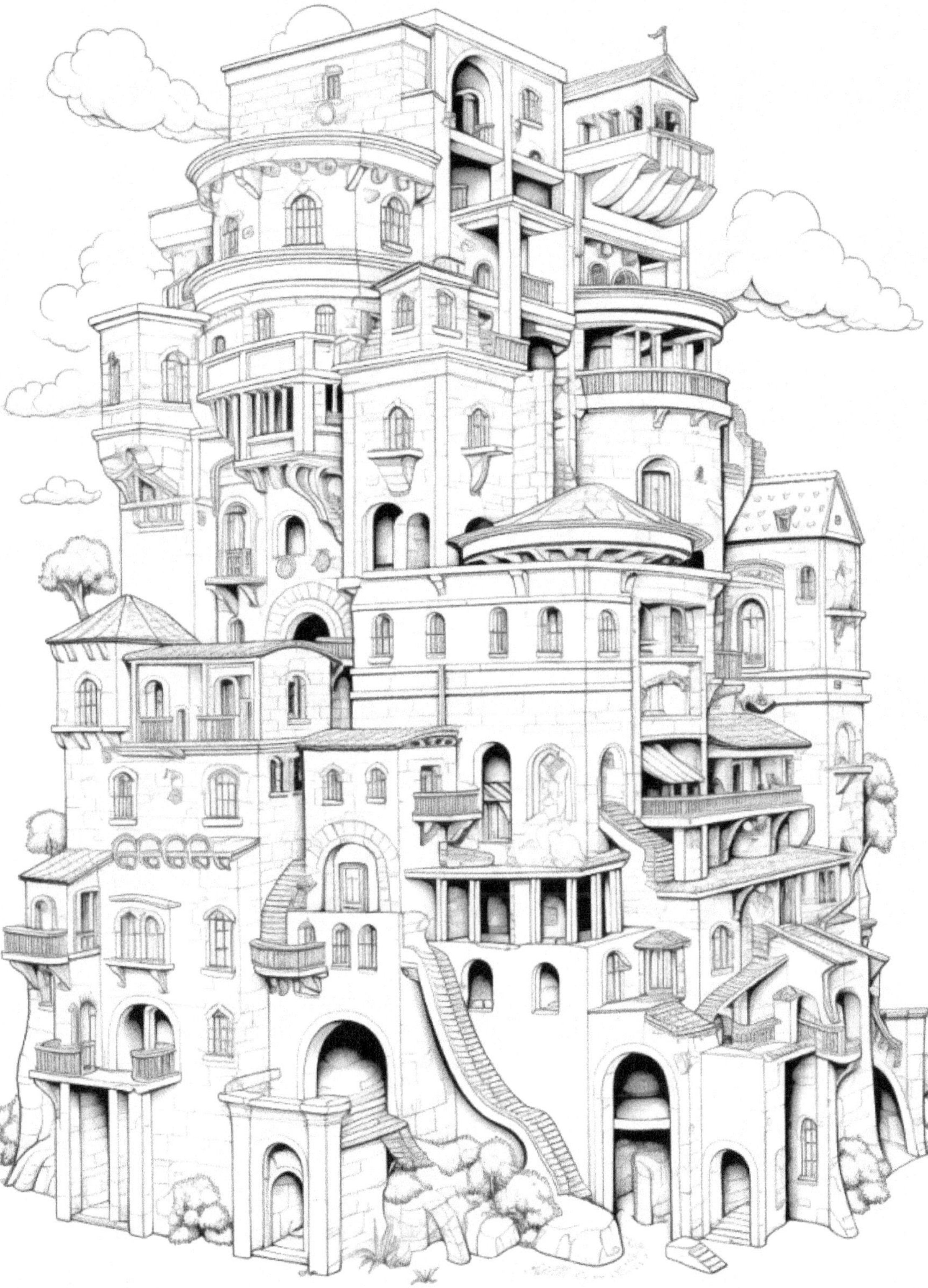

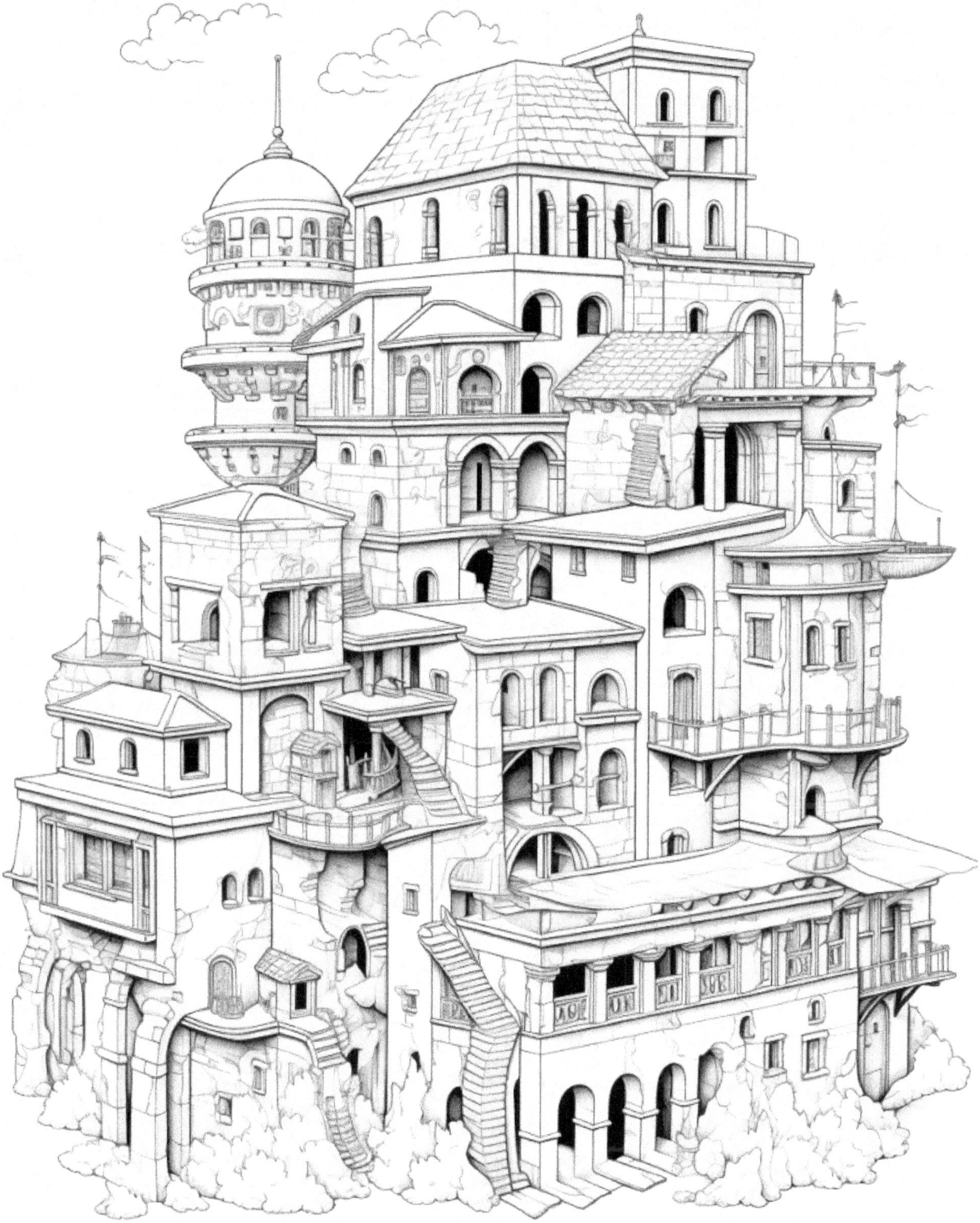

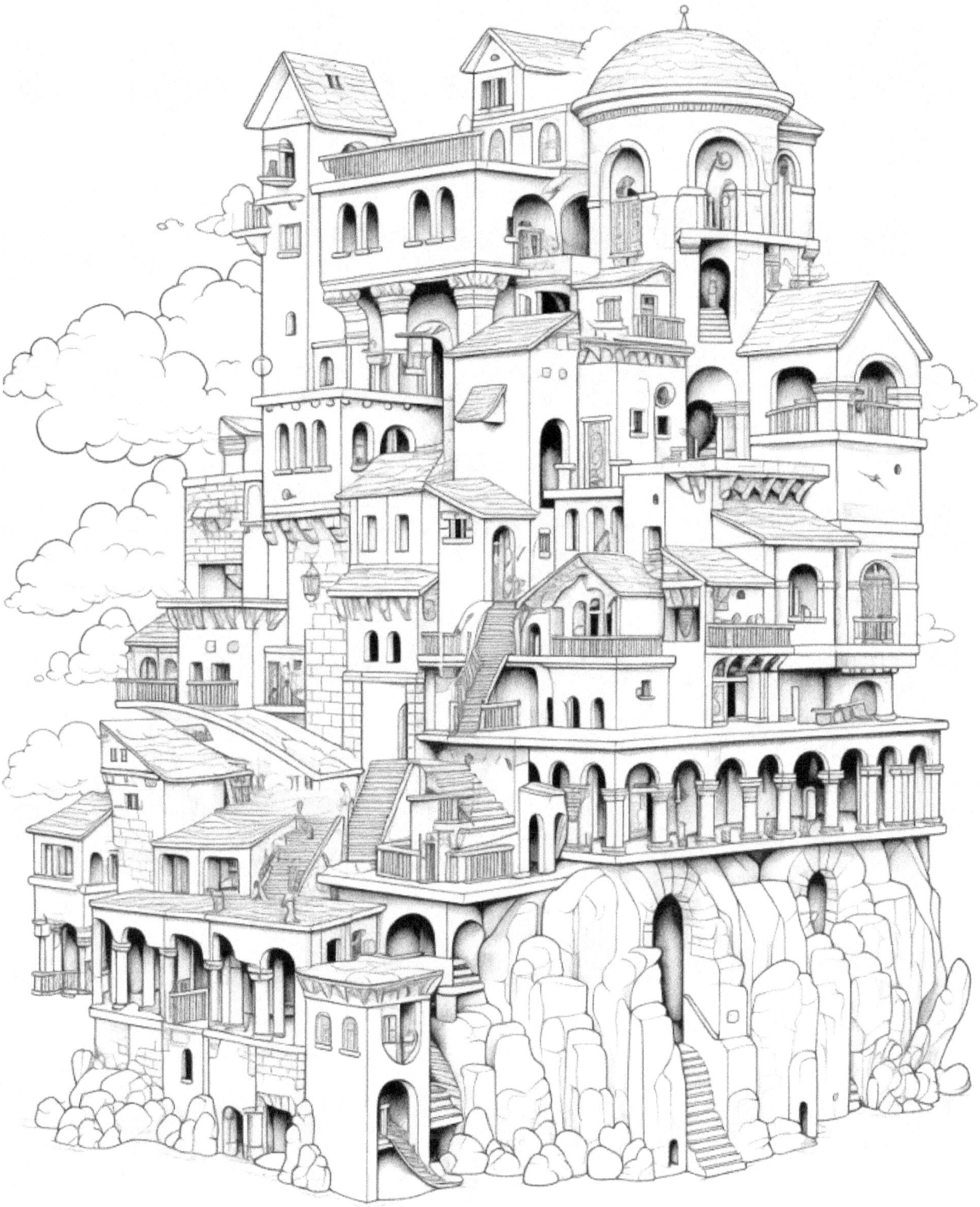

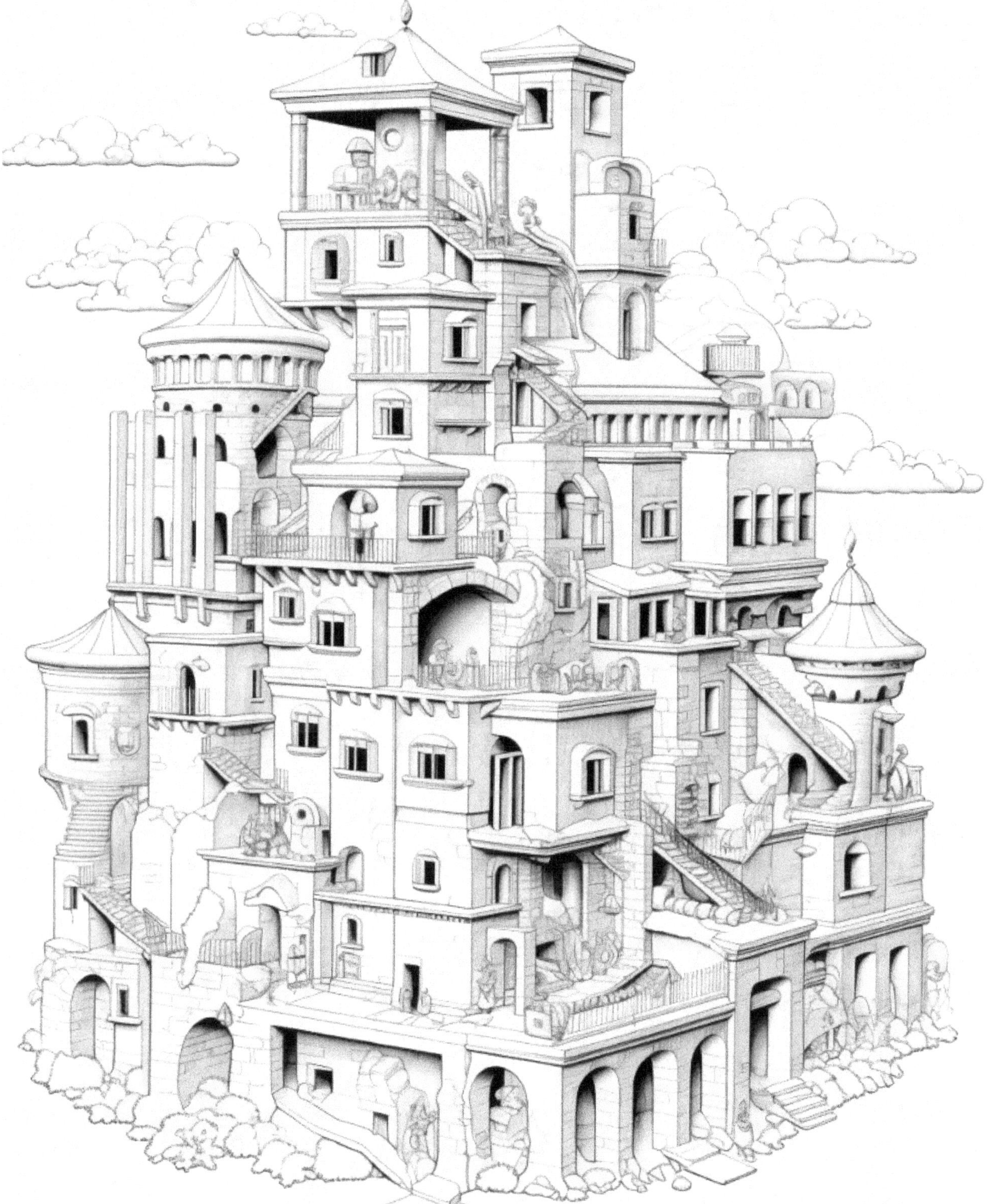

www.ingramcontent.com/pod-product-compliance
Lightning Source LLC
Chambersburg PA
CBHW082223290526
45794CB00009B/3656
* 9 7 9 8 8 5 6 4 0 3 7 5 5 *